Film and Video Resources for International Educational Exchange

SST Office
Goshen College
Goshen, IN 46526

Goshen College
Goshen, IN 46526

SST Office
bestion Toledo
English, IN 46356

Film and Video Resources for International Educational Exchange

Second Edition

Lee Zeigler

Intercultural Press, Inc.

For information contact:
Intercultural Press, Inc.
PO Box 700
Yarmouth, Maine 04096 USA
207-846-5168
www.interculturalpress.com

© 1992 by NAFSA: Association of International Educators,
© 2000 by Intercultural Press

Design and production by Patty J. Topel

All rights reserved. No part of this publication may be reproduced in any manner whatsoever without written permission from the publisher, except in the case of brief quotations embodied in critical articles or reviews.

Printed in the United States of America

04   03   02   01   00   1   2   3   4   5

Library of Congress Cataloging-in-Publication Data

Zeigler, Lee.
Film and video resources for international educational exchange/Lee Zeigler.—
2nd ed.
    p.   cm.
ISBN 1-877864-78-1
    1. Motion pictures in education.   2. Multicultural education—Film cata-
logs.   I. Title.
LB1044.Z45 2000
070.1'8—dc21   00-026785

Table of Contents

What This Directory Includes, and Why

In 1992 the first edition of *Film and Video Resources for International Educational Exchange* was published by NAFSA: Association of International Educators. Although the new version has many new entries and a number of deletions, the descriptions cited in the first edition remain valid.

This directory is designed for those who work in the many fields collectively identified as international educational exchange. This includes advisers and administrators responsible for orienting those new to the United States as students, scholars, or spouses, whether in the country for finite periods or as new immigrants. Many of the programs listed are produced as tools in learning English as a second language (E.S.L.), though some also incorporate extensive orientation to the country—in certain cases, to specific cities. Other E.S.L. programs deal with issues involving American law and social customs.

A number of the listings will be useful in preparing U.S. students going overseas. Intercultural communication, transcending all international educational exchange activity, is featured in many of the programs. Community workers who prepare volunteers for hosting international students and short-term visitors will also find helpful audiovisual training tools. Some of the listings are intended for professional development, such as sharpening E.S.L. teaching methodology and improving communication skills among university teaching assistants from foreign countries.

My motivation for assembling this directory came from personal satisfaction in using slide shows and 16 mm films—later videos—in orientation activities and ongoing campus programming during my years as director of a university-based international center. At the same time I found that locating effective materials was a time-consuming challenge, as the sources were diverse and in many cases relatively unknown. On conducting a nationwide survey of my colleagues, I learned that few of them used more than a handful of films and videos in their work, and these were essentially limited to several well-known titles.

Establishing criteria for inclusion created some challenges. Documentary and feature films dealing with specific cultures run to the tens of thousands. Anyone wishing to identify resources about one country or group of people can turn to media libraries as well as information and cultural offices of other countries and can uncover many distributors of international films. This directory is composed of materials that describe the United States, show cultural differences or cultures in conflict, or deal with multiculturalism or E.S.L. instruction in some other way. In some instances, diverse cultures in the United States are examined if the messages are relevant to the field of international educational exchange.

Some of the documentaries were produced for other audiences. Many useful products were made to train corporate personnel who are about to serve their companies overseas; others were intended for those in the workplace who deal with new immigrants. As the reader will see, distributors are many and diverse. Verification of details and availability of films involved hundreds of communications. Unfortunately, audiovisual materials are continually produced and as frequently withdrawn from circulation. I therefore apologize for any inaccuracies of information.

I am grateful to Marilyn Herand for her assistance in locating many of the titles newly listed in this edition.

Nearly all of the directory listings are produced and distributed in the United States, but a few are from other countries. You should be aware that there are several different television standards under which videos are produced. NTSC is the system used in the United States, Canada, Mexico, Central America, the Caribbean, and Japan. PAL is used in Great Britain, Australia, New Zealand, Germany, Spain, Italy, and Scandinavia. SECAM is used in France and the former USSR. Some distributors will provide videos in the standard of the recipient country if requested. If a video received in the United States is made in a standard other than NTSC, it can be converted. Some university media centers have that capability. Alternatively, some VCRs have the capacity to play videos in more than one standard automatically.

The distributor given for a particular item may not be the exclusive source. Some programs are available through a number of media centers, and costs may vary according to distributor.

Documentary Films

In part one, each documentary film listing includes title, year of release, length, formats available, description, and distributor, including address, phone number, and fax and e-mail when available. Some of the formats cited in the first directory are no longer in common use, specifically Beta and ³/₄ U-matic videos, slide shows, and filmstrips. VHS is the overwhelming format of choice, but in some cases the 16 mm film option is still available.

Cost of purchase and/or rental was deliberately excluded, because there are endless variations, such as differential rates for nonprofit organizations, and in some instances a preview showing can be negotiated at a lower rate than rental or purchase cost. In other cases the only expense of borrowing a video may be the cost of handling.

The descriptions are just that—descriptive. I have made no attempt to review or judge products as to the quality or appropriateness for a particular audience.

In addition to the alphabetical presentation, I have included a listing of documentary titles by category in the Appendix.

In part two the listing of feature films represents a selection of significant productions from around the world that focus on encounters across cultures. Many of these films are available from popular video stores; others may be located through video mail-order services. As in the case of documentaries, listing has been limited to those films that deal with conflicts arising from cross-cultural situations. There are endless numbers of films, made in other countries, that portray the specific cultures of those countries. They are useful in training students and others intending to go overseas, or in working with nationals from a specific area. Such films can be identified by country category through film catalogues and databases.

Using Long Documentary and Feature-Length Films

Films are clearly used in a variety of educational ways. Resources from this directory may be educating an audience about a new culture or a specific aspect of that culture; they may be employed to break down cultural stereotypes, to stimulate discussion on cross-cultural issues, or to deal with both verbal and nonverbal means of communication. There may be a constraint on the length of time available for a media showing. Many cross-cultural educators have found that selecting a segment—a critical incident—in a full-length film, particularly a feature film, will serve to illustrate the lesson. In previewing a film, look for the incident or situation and identify the place it occurs, so that your audience may benefit from that segment without your using class or meeting time for the entire showing.

Other Resources

NICEM Net is an online community service for those who use media and technology in education. It accesses every variety of media in addition to videos and includes information on audiovisual products and their distributors. Materials in NICEM's media archives date from 1900 to the present. Since subscription to its catalogues is rather costly, I recommend accessing the service through your local library. For more information, consult its Website: www.nicem.com. It can also be contacted at PO Box 8640, Albuquerque, NM 87198-8640; phone: 800-926-8328; fax: 505-998-3372; e-mail: nicemnet@nicem.com

Bowker's Complete Video Directory, in four volumes, contains listings for entertainment and for education and special interests. Titles are listed alphabetically, but there are also subject indexes and complete information on distributors. It is updated annually.

The Video Source Book, in two volumes, is another useful library reference, giving information on videos listed alphabetically and by subject. It is reissued periodically, with update supplements in between.

Crossing Cultures through Film, by Ellen Summerfield, was published in 1993, but the topics addressed are relevant at any time. The book is highly recommended to anyone wishing to utilize film effectively in cross-cultural instruction. More than seventy classic films, both documentary and feature, are analyzed and discussed. Topics include: how to find and evaluate films, how to use cross-cultural films, unlearning stereotypes, verbal and nonverbal communication, international conflicts, cultures within the United States, and succeeding across cultures. The book is available from Intercultural Press, PO Box 700, Yarmouth, ME 04096; phone: 800-370-2665; fax: 207-846-5181; Website: www.interculturalpress.com

Turned-on Advising, by Edward A. Riedinger, published in 1995, is a compendium of computer and video information for educational advising. It goes beyond videos to computer resources, such as CD-ROMs, floppy disks, and the Internet. Although the book is particularly designed for U.S. overseas educational advisers, it contains information of use to all who seek resources in international and intercultural education. The book is available from NAFSA Publications, PO Box 1020, Sewickley, PA 15143; phone: 800-836-4994; fax: 412-741-0609.

Leonard Maltin's Movie and Video Guide is probably the most comprehensive listing of U.S. and international feature films, covering approximately 20,000 titles, with an indication of those available on video. It also includes a useful listing of mail-order sources for video. The book is published annually as a Signet paperback and is available at most bookstores.

Home Film Festival is one of many video mail-order services, but is particularly recommended because it specializes in foreign and cross-cultural titles. It can be reached at PO Box 2032, Scranton, PA 18501; phone: 800-258-3456; fax: 717-344-3810.

A Million and One World-Wide Videos is a company that specializes in tracking hard-to-find feature and documentary films. Its sources include old film/video archives and a network of specialized collectors all over the world. It is located at PO Box 349, Orchard Hill, GA 30266-0349; phone: 800-849-7309.

102 Very Teachable Films, by Elizabeth A. Mejia, suggests popular and classic movies for E.S.L. teachers to use in their classrooms. Each film has a plot summary, a general commentary highlighting the features that are appropriate for classroom use, and suggested reading, writing, listening, speaking, and research activities. There is a subject index. The guide is available from Alta Book Center Publishers, 14 Adrian Court, Burlingame, CA 94010; phone: 800-258-2375.

Documentary Films

A-M-E-R-I-C-A-N-S
1977; 12 mins.; VHS

This film consists of interviews with several foreign-born American children who comment on how they feel about being Americans, their own origins, racial biases, and intercultural friendships.

Churchill Films, 6677 N. Northwest Highway, Chicago, IL 60631
P: 800-334-7830; F: 773-775-5091

Abortion: Stories from North to South
1984; 55 mins.; VHS

This historical overview shows how church, state, and the medical establishment have determined policies concerning abortion. From this cross-cultural survey—filmed in Ireland, Japan, Thailand, Peru, Colombia, and Canada—emerges one reality: only a small percentage of the world's women has access to a safe, legal abortion.

Cinema Guild, 1697 Broadway, New York, NY 10019
P: 212-246-5522; F: 212-246-5525; e-mail: thecinemag@aol.com

Accent Reduction
1993-1996; 40 to 56 mins. each; VHS

This is a correction series of five films for speakers of English whose first language is Arabic, Japanese, Korean, Chinese, or Thai. Each individual program deals with the different sounds of English consonants and vowels, problem consonants and consonant clusters, problem vowels, syllable and word stress, and blending. Through animation, close-ups, and humorous vignettes, the learning experience is made effective.

Crossroads Video, 15 Buckminster Lane, Manhasset, NY 10030
P: 516-365-3715; F: 516-365-3715; e-mail: crossrds@linet.com

Across Cultures
1983; 15 mins. each; VHS

This series is designed to introduce students to the concept of culture and help them appreciate cultures that are vastly different from their own. Individual titles include *The Japanese, The Tarahomara, The Baoole, Providing for Family Needs, The Environment, Religion, Passing on Tradition, Education, Sports, Society and*

Self, Communication, Cultural Exchange, Cultural Change, and *Choices for the Future.*

Agency for Instructional Technology, 1800 N. Stonelake Drive, Bloomington, IN 47404

P: 800-457-4509; F: 812-333-4278; e-mail: ait@ait.net

Acting Our Age

1993; 30 mins.; VHS

Residents of a senior home for South Asians interview people on the street, showing cross-cultural values and intergenerational attitudes, as well as everyday problems of some elderly.

NAATA Distribution, 346 Ninth Street, 2nd Floor, San Francisco, CA 94103

P: 415-552-9550; F: 415-863-7428; e-mail: naata@sirius.com

Adjustment to a New Way of Life

1989; 22 mins.; VHS

Many newcomers, especially Southeast Asians, come from societies fundamentally different in philosophy, religion, politics, and social structure. This program takes a close look at four refugees from different countries and varied backgrounds. They each discuss difficulties they faced as new members of American society and how they have learned to cope in their new environment. (Part of the Newcomers to America series; available in fifteen languages.)

Newcomers to America, PO Box 339, Portland, OR 97207

P: 800-776-1610

AFS Diversity Initiative, The

1999; 14 mins.; VHS

The American Field Service Diversity Recruitment Initiative is presented in the context of its history and mission. AFS returnees from diverse backgrounds and their parents talk about the experience of going abroad with AFS. Students participated in programs in Ghana, Venezuela, Latvia, and China. The video also extends an invitation to families from diverse backgrounds to consider hosting a student from abroad.

AFS Intercultural Programs, Marketing Dept., 198 Madison Avenue, 8th Floor, New York, NY 10016

P: 212-299-9000, ext. 340; F: 212-299-9090

AFS Experience, The: Parent Focus

1998; 20 mins.; VHS

This video comprises the material found in *The AFS Experience: Student Focus*, but contains four additional minutes of parent-directed material added by the parents of the four returnees.

AFS Intercultural Programs, Marketing Dept., 198 Madison Avenue, 8th Floor, New York, NY 10016

P: 212-299-9000, ext. 340; F: 212-299-9090

AFS Experience, The: Student Focus

1998; 16 mins.; VHS

The American Field Service experience is seen through the eyes of four U.S. returnees and their parents. Lisa (Sweden), Reid (France), Rachel (Russia), and Michael (Japan) and their parents talk about their AFS experiences and what they meant to them. Basic questions about this high school exchange program as it operates in other countries are answered.

AFS Intercultural Programs, Marketing Dept., 198 Madison Avenue, 8th Floor, New York, NY 10016

P: 212-299-9000, ext. 340; F: 212-299-9090

After America...After Japan

1999; 4 hours; VHS

This five-part series examines the experience of coming home for Americans who have lived in Japan and for Japanese who have lived in America. It features academics, corporate executives, attorneys, musicians, and an ordained Buddhist priest. The African American experience is highlighted by a couple who gave up law careers in the U.S. to spend nine years studying traditional Japanese musical instruments. There is also a 2-hour version, and a 22-minute derivative version for K-12.

Doubles Film Library, 22-D Hollywood Avenue, Hohokus, NJ 07423

P: 800-343-5540; F: 201-652-1973

After the Cult: Recovering Together

1994; 25 mins.; VHS

Ten ex-cult members talk about their experiences in cults and their recovery from the experiences. They discuss how recruiters deceived, manipulated, and pressured them into joining and staying in their cults, how these experiences affected them, and how they are coping with their strong feelings of rage and pain. This is a supplement to an earlier production, *Cults: Saying No under Pressure*.

American Family Foundation/International Cult Education Program, PO Box 1232, Gracie Station, New York, NY 10028

P: 212-533-5420; F: 212-533-0538

Afterbirth

1982; 34 mins.; VHS

American-born Asians explore the relationship between their "internal" and "external" selves–the pressure to be Asian and/or American.

NAATA Distribution, 346 Ninth Street, 2nd Floor, San Francisco, CA 94103

P: 415-522-9550; F: 415-863-7428; e-mail: naata@sirius.com

All Dressed in White

1994; 18 mins.; VHS

Four women in a Catholic Indian family each marry in a different place and a different era, from Goa to California. The film shows the dilemmas that each dealt with in choosing her wedding dress and for carving out her cultural identity in relation to Europeans, Americans, and other Indians.

Center for Media and Independent Learning, 2000 Center Street, 4th Floor, Berkeley, CA 94704

P: 510-642-0460; F: 510-643-9271; e-mail: cmil@uclink.berkeley.edu

American Business English

1987; 75 mins. each; VHS

This series of eight video-based English courses centers on natural English as it is used by American businesspeople in everyday working life. The course level progresses from low-intermediate to advanced and is composed of fourteen case studies presented in forty 15-minute programs. Each case study covers a particular industry or business activity, such as: market research, retailing, banking, manufacturing, electronics, telemarketing, hotels, etc.

Pace Group International, 2020 S.W. 4th Avenue, 7th Floor, Portland, OR 97201

P: 503-226-7223; F: 503-224-7413; e-mail: pacevideo@aol.com

American Game: Japanese Rules

1988; 60 mins.; VHS

Several scenarios of Americans living and working in Japan raise questions about intercultural interactions, such as respect for each other's rules and accommodation by one side to another. The film asks what Americans can learn from dealing with the Japanese.

PBS Video, 1320 Braddock Place, Alexandria, VA 22314-1698

P: 800-344-3337; F: 703-739-5269

American Scenes

1985; 60 mins. each; VHS

Short skits are grouped in seven thematic areas on seven tapes: travel, housing, food, university life, emergency situations, everyday living, and social settings. The programs are structural/situational, with more than 350 idioms and colloquial expressions. Workbooks and a teacher's manual are included. Bilingual (Spanish/English).

Crossroads Video, Inc., 15 Buckminster Lane, Manhasset, NY 11030

P: 516-365-3715; F: 516-365-3715; e-mail: crossrds@linet.com

American Tongues

1987; 56 mins.; VHS

This video portrays some of the interesting regional, social, and ethnic differences in American speech and the attitudes that people have about these differences. It is intended to educate viewers about the nature of dialects, and it also challenges them to confront their own attitudes about language variation.

Iowa State University Instructional Technology Center, 1200 Communication Building, Ames, IA 50011

P: 800-447-0060; F: 515-294-8089

Anatomy of a Spring Roll

1994; 56 mins.; VHS

The Vietnamese-born immigrant tells of finding his new life in America, while keeping the connection with his homeland through cooking, eating, and sharing the foods of Vietnam. The undercurrent of the film is his longing for his homeland. When his father dies in Vietnam, he returns and is finally able to reconcile memory with reality.

Filmakers Library, Inc., 124 East 40th Street, New York, NY 10016

P: 212-808-4980; F: 212-808-4983; e-mail: info@filmakers.com

Applying for the F-1 Student Visa at an American Consulate

1995; 60 mins.; VHS

The presenters use specific examples and case scenarios to address a number of troubling and confusing questions in the student visa application process. The seemingly arbitrary process becomes understandable once the underlying legal concerns and philosophy are understood.

Immigration Educational Services, 6300 Wilshire Boulevard, Suite 1010, Los Angeles, CA 90048-5204

P: 213-966-4980

Authentic American Activities
1983; 60 mins. each; VHS

Intermediate to advanced learners are provided with valuable listening comprehension and speaking practice. The series of three tapes combines cultural information with an opportunity to work with the unscripted, natural conversation of
real people (not actors) in a variety of entertaining settings.
Pace Group International, 2020 S.W. 4th Avenue, 7th Floor, Portland, OR 97201
P: 503-226-7223; F: 503-224-7413; e-mail: pacevideo@aol.com

Balablok
1972; 8 mins.; 16 mm; VHS

This classic film, using images alone without commentary, reduces human conflict to simple forms. Animated blocks squeak friendly greetings as they walk
past each other. Startled by a strange shape, a ball, they taunt it. Both sides call up
reserves. Balls and blocks batter each other until all are uniformly hexagonal and
friends. Then a triangle walks in!
Encyclopaedia Britannica, 310 S. Michigan Avenue, Chicago, IL 60604
P: 800-554-9862; F: 312-294-2138

Be Good, My Children
1992; 47 mins.; 16 mm; VHS

A humorous drama about a Korean immigrant family in New York City, whose
members each have very different ideas about what life should be like in their
adopted homeland. The story revolves around the conflict between a hardworking,
religious mother and her two headstrong children.
Women Make Movies, 462 Broadway, 5th Floor, New York, NY 10013
P: 212-925-0606; F: 212-925-2052

Becoming American
1982; 58 mins. (also 30 mins. version); 16 mm; VHS

A Hmong tribal family from Laos journey to the U.S. after many years in a Thai
refugee camp. Life in Seattle brings the family face-to-face with intense culture
shock and prejudice before they gradually adapt.
New Day Films, 22-D Hollywood Avenue, Hohokus, NJ 07423
P: 201-652-6590; F: 201-652-1973; e-mail: tmcndy@aol.com

Before You Pack: Preparing for Study in Africa
1999; 30 mins.; VHS

This video assists the prospective traveler in dealing with the immediate necessi-
ties and the deeper issues of how to prepare for studying in Africa. Topics include

predeparture arrangements, pertinent information gathering, travel documentation and health issues, and culture shock.

NCSA, African Studies Center, Michigan State University, 100 International Center, East Lansing, MI 48824-1035

P: 517-353-1700; F: 517-432-1209: e-mail: ncsa@pilot.msu.edu

Better Together Than A-P-A-R-T

1996; 62 mins.; VHS

Dr. Milton Bennett outlines the basic concepts of intercultural communication, presents the development of an intercultural sensitivity, and discusses what it takes to be interculturally competent.

Intercultural Resource Corporation, 78 Greylock Road, Newtonville, MA 02460

P: 617-965-8651; F: 617-969-7347; e-mail: info@irc-international.com

Between Two Worlds: The Hmong Shaman in America

1985; 30 mins.; VHS

The lives of the Hmong refugees in America are described. Though transferred from their mountain home in Laos to high-rise tenements in the U.S., they have brought their ancient rituals and ceremonies to urban America. The filmmaker points out the similarities in beliefs between the Hmong and Native Americans.

Filmakers Library, Inc., 124 East 40th Street, New York, NY 10016

P: 212-808-4980; F: 212-808-4983; e-mail: info@filmakers.com

Bias Awareness in a Multicultural World

1991; 50 mins.; VHS

This two-tape video set (each 25 minutes) focuses on bias, prejudice, and racism. Experts from higher education offer diverse insights, strategies, and techniques that students can use to be successful in a multicultural world.

College Survival, Inc., 2650 Jackson Boulevard, Rapid City, SD 57702-3474

P: 800-528-8323

Bittersweet Survival

1981; 30 mins.; 16 mm; VHS

This film examines resettlement problems of Southeast Asian refugees, including the hostilities and frustration they experience. Immigration policy as it relates to political policy over the decade of the 1970s is also explored.

Third World Newsreel, 335 W. 38th Street, 3rd Floor, New York, NY 10018

P: 212-947-9277; F: 212-594-6417; e-mail: twn@twn.org

Bittersweet: The Asian-Indian Experience in the USA

1995; 42 mins.; VHS

Asian-Indian immigrants in the U.S. discuss the complex social and personal issues involved in dealing with dual cultural influences. The film illuminates the issue of cultural identity and the problems of defining community in an adopted land.

The Cinema Guild, Inc., 1697 Broadway, Suite 506, New York, NY 10019-5904
P: 800-723-5522; F: 212-246-5525; e-mail: thecinemag@aol.com

Black to the Promised Land

1992; 95 mins.; VHS

This is the story of eleven black American teenagers, who, with their Jewish teacher, travel from their homes in the Bedford-Stuyvesant section of Brooklyn to Israel, where they spend several months living and working as members of a kibbutz. After a vivid portrait of the teens at home and at school in Brooklyn, we witness the unfolding of their Israeli experience as they confront an alien culture, people, and way of life. We also see the effects of this experience after they resume life in the inner city.

First Run/Icarus Films, 153 Waverly Place, 6th Floor, New York, NY 10014
P: 212-727-1711; F: 212-255-7923; e-mail: mail@frif.com

Blue-Collar and Buddha

1988; 57 mins.; VHS

This dramatic documentary explores the arrival of Laotian refugees into a small Midwestern blue-collar town. Townspeople frustrated by economic depression and angry about having lost the Vietnam War confront proud immigrants intent on preserving their culture and Buddhist religion. This was the winner of many film festival awards.

Filmakers Library, Inc., 124 East 40th Street, New York, NY 10016
P: 212-808-4980; F: 212-808-4983

Blue-Eyed

1995; 93 mins.; VHS

This video shows a workshop with diversity trainer Jane Elliott, whose 1968 blue-eyed/brown-eyed exercise was a groundbreaking experiment in anti-racist training. The participants are forty teachers, police, school administrators, and social workers. The blue-eyed members are subjected to pseudoscientific explanations of their inferiority, culturally based I.Q. tests, and religious discrimination.

California Newsreel, 149 Ninth Street, #420, San Francisco, CA 94103
P: 415-621-6196; F: 415-621-6522; e-mail: newsreel@ix.netcom.com

Body Language: An International View

1999; 23 mins.; VHS

This film highlights gestures, facial expressions, and nuances in body language across cultures. It takes a humorous yet informative look at a variety of global styles in nonverbal communication and is designed for cultural training, intensive English programs, foreign student orientation, and use by international agencies.

The Seabright Group, Instructional Media, 216 F Street, Suite 25, Davis, CA 95616 P/F: 530-759-0684; e-mail: SeabrightG@davis.com

Bonds of Pride, The

1991; 28 mins.; VHS

This program explores the nature of the Arab identity and the main cultural ties that hold the Arab world together. Cultural diversity among various Arab groups is examined, along with the role of women in Islamic society.

Films for the Humanities and Sciences, PO Box 2053, Princeton, NJ 08543-2053 P: 800-257-5126; F: 609-275-3767; e-mail: custserv@films.com

Breaking the Accent Barrier

1991; 60 mins.; VHS

This video features Dr. David Stern, dialect coach, instructing speech pathologists and E.S.L. teachers in his accent-reduction techniques. In nine sequential lessons, the video teaches the American style of intonation, muscularity, voice placement, and tongue movement.

Video Language Products, PO Box 641, South Pasadena, CA 91031-0641 P: 800-367-3806; F: 626-799-4729; e-mail: info@videolanguage.com

Brighter Moon, A

1986; 25 mins.; 16 mm; VHS

This dramatized tale is about two Hong Kong students who confront their dreams for a better life through getting an education in Canada.

Wondrous Light, Inc., 174 Fulton Avenue, Toronto, ON M4K 1Y3, Canada P: 416-429-7399; F: 416-696-9108; e-mail: klock@pathcom.com

Building Bridges to Friendship

1989; 20 mins.; VHS

This video from Macalester College was produced for use in orientation of new international students in the U.S.; U.S. students going to study abroad; E.S.L. students; college personnel in counseling, advising, and programming; and cross-cultural communication students.

NAFSA Publications, PO Box 1020, Sewickley, PA 15143 P: 800-836-4994; F: 412-741-0609; e-mail: inbox@nafsa.org

Building the Transnational Team

1993; 25 mins.; VHS

This program focuses on the critical issue of how to create productive teams in a multicultural environment. It follows a team of managers from five different countries, revealing the cross-cultural and communication pitfalls they encounter. Each manager reveals his or her cultural mindset and how he or she learned to deal with various issues in a transnational team.

Big World Inc., 4204 Tamarack Court, Suite 100, Boulder, CO 80304

P: 800-682-1261; F: 303-444-6190; e-mail: bigworld@aol.com

Chairy Tale, A

1957; 10 mins.; 16 mm; VHS

This classic black-and-white animated film, a modern fairy tale without words in the form of a simple ballet, depicts a chair that declines to be sat upon and a young man attempting to sit on it. It is a production of film artist Norman McLaren, with musical accompaniment by Ravi Shankar and Chatur Lal. It is used as a metaphor for cultural interaction.

International Film Bureau, Inc., 332 S. Michigan Avenue, Chicago, IL 60604-4382

P: 800-432-2241

Chief in Two Worlds, A

1993; 52 mins.; VHS

A Samoan chieftain living in Los Angeles undergoes his formal induction ceremony in Samoa, followed by a view of his new role when he returns to Los Angeles. It is a study of his coming to terms with two societies and an examination of cultural change and resilience.

Center for Media and Independent Learning, 2000 Center Street, 4th Floor, Berkeley, CA 94704

P: 510-642-0460; F: 510-643-9271; e-mail: cmil@uclink.berkeley.edu

Chinese Cultural Values: The Other Pole of the Human Mind

1996; 60 mins.; VHS

A Chinese woman discusses her childhood, family, interpersonal relationships, and work, including her experiences in the U.S. and with Americans. Dr. George Renwick interprets these remarks to better understand not only the Chinese but ourselves as well.

Intercultural Resource Corporation, 78 Greylock Road, Newtonville, MA 02460

P: 617-965-8651; F: 617-969-7347; e-mail: info@irc-international.com

Class Divided, A

1985; 60 mins.; VHS

An updated version of the 1970 documentary *The Eye of the Storm*, this program of the PBS Frontline series reviews a daring lesson attempted in 1968 to introduce the concept of prejudice into a third-grade classroom. It utilizes footage from scenes at a reunion of the former third-graders and includes reflections by the teacher to illustrate this unique classroom and to examine and update the results.

PBS Video, 1320 Braddock Place, Alexandria, VA 22314

P: 800-344-3337; F: 703-739-5269

Clothing—A Cross-Cultural Study, Parts 1 and 2

1990; 32 mins.; VHS

This revised program examines factors that affect clothing, including climate, age, status, sex, job, and fashion. It looks at clothing materials and the many ways people make and take care of clothing.

Educational Design, 245 Hudson Street, New York, NY 10014

P: 800-221-9372; F: 212-675-6922

Cold Water

1987; 48 mins.; VHS

The intercultural adjustment process of international students at an American university is explored, emphasizing that at the core of this adjustment process is the conflict of foreign values with the American value system. Topics include privacy, openness/directness, attitudes toward time, friendship patterns, informality, and competitiveness.

Intercultural Press, PO Box 700, Yarmouth ME 04096

P: 800-370-2665; F: 207-846-5181; e-mail: books@interculturalpress.com

College Students and AIDS

1989; 26 mins.; 16 mm; VHS

The film's content, presented as a discussion among university students of many ethnic groups, intends to help students identify and overcome the social and psychological barriers surrounding AIDS and enable them to lower their risk of becoming infected.

Center for Media and Independent Learning, 2000 Center Street, 4th Floor, Berkeley, CA 94704

P: 510-642-0460; F: 510-643-9271; e-mail: cmil@uclink.berkeley.edu

Color of Fear, The

1994; 90 mins.; VHS

This film describes the state of race relations in America as seen through the eyes of eight men of various ethnicities. The effects that racism has had on each of them are seen from a psychosocial viewpoint. One by one, the men reveal the pain and scars that racism has caused them, the defense mechanisms they use to survive, their fears of each other, and their hopes and visions for a multicultural society.

Stir-Fry Seminars and Consulting, Inc., 3345 Grand Avenue, Suite 3, Oakland, CA 94610

P: 510-419-3930; F: 510-419-3934

Color Schemes

1989; 28 mins.; VHS

In looking at America's multicultural society, the film uses the metaphor of "color wash" to tackle conceptions of racial assimilation. Twelve writer/performers spin through this tumble-jumble of America's washload, scheming to claim racial images that remain in vivid color.

Women Make Movies, 462 Broadway, 5th Floor, New York, NY 10013

P: 212-925-0606; F: 212-925-2052

Columbus on Trial

1993; 18 mins.; VHS

Inspired by the controversy surrounding the five hundredth anniversary of Columbus' discovery of America, a fanciful version of a courtroom shows Columbus returning from his grave to stand trial. Cross-examined by the Latino comedy group, Culture Clash, Columbus is charged with atrocities against the Native peoples of the New World.

Women Make Movies, 462 Broadway, 5th Floor, New York, NY 10013

P: 212-925-0606; F: 212-925-2052

Coming Across

1989; 46 mins.; VHS

Five South Los Angeles students interview new immigrants from Central America, Southest Asia, Mexico, Iran, and the former Soviet Union, attempting to learn whether their dreams of freedom from oppression or poverty are realized or if they suffer disappointment and disillusionment. This two-part video explores reasons for immigration, differences and discoveries in education, resources and skills in transition, and recovery from wartime trauma and disruption.

Pyramid Film and Video, PO Box 1048, Santa Monica, CA 90406-1048

P: 800-421-2304; F: 310-453-9083; e-mail: info@pyramedia.com

Communicating Survival

1986-91; 15-30 mins. each; VHS

This series of seven programs teaches immigrants and refugees about vital public services in the U.S.: *Emergency—Call 911; Help Wanted; Personal Checking; The Supermarket; Obtaining Health Care; It's the Law;* and *Tenant Orientation.* Tapes are available in Amharic, English, Farsi, Khmer, Korean, Lao, Spanish, Tigringa, and Vietnamese.

Arlington Community Television, 3401 N. Fairfax Drive, Suite 300, Arlington, VA 22201

P: 703-524-2388; F: 703-908-9239

Conversational Style in the USA

1996; 75 mins.; VHS

This two-section video takes the viewer through twelve steps of learning the "basketball conversational style" widely used in the U.S. These procedures include back channeling, interrupting politely, using hesitation techniques, and so forth. It is accompanied by a conversational inventory and a written assessment tool that calculates personal conversational style and relates the score to international patterns. Part of the Fluent American English series.

The Seabright Group, Instructional Media, 216 F Street, Suite 25, Davis, CA 95616

P/F: 530-759-0684; e-mail: SeabrightG@davis.com

Conversational Styles around the Globe

1996; 36 mins.; VHS

Using the metaphor of three popular sports, the video highlights differences in conversational styles found around the world, corresponding to features of pacing, volume, topic changes, level of participation, turn taking, and rapport among speakers. Part of the Fluent American English series.

The Seabright Group, Instructional Media, 216 F Street, Suite 25, Davis, CA 95616

P/F: 530-759-0684; e-mail: SeabrightG@davis.com

Corporate Warrior

1993; 30 mins.; VHS

The variety of Japanese and American cultural issues, Japanese and American divergent views of the world, and the individual and general differences between traditional and modern ways of dealing with life, love, and death are examined. The relationship between a Japanese woman and her pregnant American daughter-in-law, as they reach across cultural biases to accept each other, forms the core of this production.

Carousel Film and Video, 280 Fifth Avenue, New York, NY 10001

P: 212-683-1660; F: 212-683-1662; e-mail: carousel@pipeline.com

Cross-Cultural Communication in Diverse Settings

1992; 60 mins.; VHS

This video discusses characteristics and elements of communication and the difficulties of communicating across cultures.

RMI Media Productions, Inc., 1365 N. Winchester, Olathe, KS 66061

P: 800-745-5480; F: 800-755-6910

Cross-Cultural Communications

1974; 40 mins.; VHS

Verbal and nonverbal languages change in different cultural environments. We are shown how nonverbal language can provide valuable insights into the culture itself.

NETCHE Inc., 1800 N. 33rd Street, Lincoln, NE 68583

P: 402-472-9333, ext. 224; F: 402-472-1785; e-mail: Idam@unlinfo.unl.edu

Cross-Cultural Comparisons

1994; 60 mins.; VHS

Hindu, Chinese, and Islamic gender roles are discussed. Cultural practices that give men absolute authority and control over women are discussed within the context of each culture.

RMI Media Productions, Inc., 1365 N. Winchester, Okathe, KS 66061

P: 800-745-5480; F: 913-362-6910

Cross-Cultural Comparisons, Continued

1994; 60 mins.; VHS

This sequel to *Cross-Cultural Comparisons* focuses on societies that have tried to change gender inequities with specific policies and changes in law. China, the former Soviet Union, and Sweden are discussed.

RMI Media Productions, Inc., 1365 N. Winchester, Okathe, KS 66061

P: 800-745-5480; F: 913-362-6910

Cross-Cultural Differences in Newborn Behavior

1980; 12 mins.; VHS

Research on newborn infants shows that there are standard differences in temperament or behavior among babies from different ethnic backgrounds and that such differences are biological as well as cultural.

Pennsylvania State University, Audio Visual Services, University Park, PA 16802

P: 800-826-0132

Cross-Cultural Problem Solving

1985; 7 hrs.; VHS

This unit in the Intercultural Communication series emphasizes the role of the "third-party helper," employing a problem-solving model which addresses the cross-cultural elements in problematic situations. The Colombian culture is featured.

Youth For Understanding Program Services, 3501 Newark Street, NW, Washington, DC 20016

P: 800-424-3691, ext. 134; F: 202-895-1104

Cross-Purposes

1986; 28 mins.; VHS

This program attempts to provide the very large picture needed to advance individual understanding of unconscious attitudes. Along with the discussion guide, it presents five vignettes in which Americans and international students confront the challenge of cross-cultural communication. Each scene is an opportunity to explore a different aspect of the foreign/U.S. or foreign/professor relationship.

Michael J. Dumas, International Student Adviser, Mills College, Oakland, CA 94613

P: 510-430-2130

Crosstalk

1982; 30 mins.; 16 mm; VHS

This British production demonstrates the many difficulties involved in interethnic verbal communication, suggesting possible solutions through practical action at the local community level. It is designed for professional people who work with ethnic minorities seeking access to wider opportunities and rights: personnel officers, supervisors, interviewers, health care providers, counselors, social workers, and others.

Center for Media and Independent Learning, 2000 Center Street, 4th Floor, Berkeley, CA 94704

P: 510-642-0460; F: 510-643-9271; e-mail: cmil@uclink.berkeley.edu

Cults: Saying No under Pressure

1990; 29 mins.; VHS

This program was designed to expose foreign students in the U.S. to the deception, psychological manipulation, and mind-control techniques used in cult recruitment and retention. It includes segments on defining cults and their effects on individuals and families, as well as an enactment of a possible cult recruitment scene. Included with the video are a discussion guide, resource guide, and bibliography.

American Family Foundation/International Cult Education Program, PO Box 1232, Gracie Station, New York, NY 10028

P: 212-533-5420; F: 212-533-0538

Cultural Baggage

1995; 8 mins.; VHS

This video uses humor to understand and prevent stereotyping behavior. It was created to parody the stereotypes with which people are often labeled. Its humorous approach draws attention to attitudes that need to be changed.

Pyramid Film and Video, PO Box 1048, Santa Monica, CA 90406-1048

P: 800-421-2304; F: 310-453-9083; e-mail: info@pyramedia.com

Cultural Crossings

1993; 55 mins.; VHS

This film about international students and the professionals who work with them is intended as an orientation tool and a discussion prompter for new advisers and other campus staff. It addresses challenges for international students, advisers, and other cross-cultural communicators.

Canadian Bureau for International Education, 220 Laurier Avenue W., Suite 1100, Ottawa, ON K1P 5Z9 Canada

P: 613-237-4820; F: 613-237-1073

Cultural Diversity: At the Heart of Bull

1992; 28 mins.; VHS

This video is designed to inform and assist people in dealing with ethnic and cultural diversity in the workplace. It focuses specifically on cultural differences between French and Americans, as seen from the perspective of Bull HN Information Systems employees. It shows how employees from both cultures perceive themselves, one another, and the world around them.

Intercultural Press, PO Box 700, Yarmouth, ME 04096

P: 800-370-2665; F: 207-846-5168; e-mail: books@interculturalpress.com

Cultural Diversity: Meeting the Challenge

1989; 20 mins.; VHS

This program, in discussing cross-cultural issues, is intended to increase resident Americans' understanding of other cultures, especially the newcomer's own social confusion about living in a strange new land. (Part of the Newcomers to America series; available in English only.)

Newcomers to America, PO Box 339; Portland, OR 97207-0339

P: 800-776-1610; F: 503-554-9117

Culture Clash and the Law in America

1989; 39 mins.; VHS

This program focuses on an actual case of a Vietnamese man charged with the murder of his girlfriend. What appears at first to be an open-and-shut case leads

the viewer through some surprising developments to its conclusion. This program is intended for judges, attorneys, interpreters, and anyone else involved with alien or non-English speaking persons in the judicial system. (Part of the Newcomers to America series; available in English only.)
Newcomers to America, PO Box 339, Portland, OR 97207-0339
P: 800-776-1610; F: 503-241-3507

Culture: What Is It?

1993; 11 mins.; VHS

Culture is defined as the sum total of the human experience, a people's whole way of life. Dividing culture into material and nonmaterial categories, on-location footage provides examples from a variety of cultures around the world. Students see and hear about similarities and differences among cultures, how people with similar background share cultural traits, and how cultural traits are passed from generation to generation.
AGC/United Learning, 1560 Sherman Avenue, Suite 100, Evanston, IL 60201
P: 800-424-0362; F: 847-647-0918; e-mail: bistern@interaccess.com

Cultures around the World

1980; 35 mins.; VHS

This comprehensive investigation of the concept of culture is based upon a study of societies from every corner of the globe. It shows how cultures reflect such factors as technology, habitat, and the borrowing of culture forms. It includes comparisons of such things as toys, tools, and even entire lifestyles, presented in terms of four technological levels: hunting and gathering, agriculture, city civilization, and industry.
Educational Design, Inc., 245 Hudson Street, New York, NY, 10014
P: 800-221-9372; F: 212-675-6922

Cultures: Similarities and Differences

1996; 20 mins.; VHS

Shot in many locations around the world, this program first identifies a common element of cultures—groups—and then shows why and how they may differ from one to another. It then explains that all cultures have different methods of expressing ideas and emotions through language and various creative and performing arts.
AGC/United Learning, 1560 Sherman Avenue, Suite 100, Evanston, IL 60201
P: 800-424-0362; F: 847-647-0918; e-mail: bistern@interaccess.com

Dance and Human History
1976; 40 mins.; 16 mm; VHS

This program introduces the work of Alan Lomax and his colleagues in developing choreometrics, a cross-cultural method of studying the relationship of dance style to social structure. It shows how the group analyzed dance films from all over the world and established a connection between patterns of movement and patterns of culture.

Center for Media and Independent Learning, 2000 Center Street, 4th Floor, Berkeley, CA 94704

P: 510-642-0460; F: 510-643-9271; e-mail: cmil@uclink.berkeley.edu

Desi Remix Chicago Style
1996; 46 mins.; VHS

This energetic film follows three very different Punjabi bands and their efforts to make music the bridge between Indian and American cultures.

Third World Newsreel, 335 West 38th Street, 5th Floor, New York, NY 10018

P: 212-947-9277; F: 212-594-6417; e-mail: twn@twn.org

Developing a Dual Perspective
1985; 6½ hrs.; VHS

Participants develop and practice skills for understanding an event, situation, issue, or relationship from the perspective of people from different cultures. The video features the interactions of a Japanese exchange student and an American family. (One of six units in the Intercultural Communication series; it can be shortened to three hours.)

Youth For Understanding Program Services, 3501 Newark Street, NW, Washington DC 20016

P: 800-424-3691, ext. 134; F: 202-895-1104

Different Place, A *and* Creating Community
1993; 37 mins.; VHS

This two-part video provides a framework for discussion of complex intercultural issues in the learning environment. *A Different Place* depicts a classroom of foreign and American students interacting with one another and with their professor. *Creating Community* provides an analysis of the drama by experts in sociology, anthropology, education, and communication.

Intercultural Resource Corporation, 78 Greylock Road, Newtonville, MA 02460

P: 617-965-8651; F: 617-969-7347; e-mail: info@irc-international.com

Direct Connection

1985; 30 mins.; VHS

This film documents the beginning of a highly successful exchange between high school students in the U.S. and the former Soviet Union that later resulted in personal meetings with President Reagan and Secretary Gorbachev. This moving program led to the adoption of similar initiatives in many Soviet and American schools and to a major exchange of high school students.

The Video Project, 200 Estates Drive, Ben Lomond, CA 95005

P: 800-4-PLANET; F: 831-336-2168; e-mail: videoproject@videoproject.org

Discrimination in the Workplace

1996; 18 mins.; VHS

Discrimination based on national origin or citizenship status is illegal. However, to many employers and employees alike, this kind of discrimination is also confusing. This program defines nationality and citizenship discrimination, how to identify it, how to deal with it when it appears, and how to get help from local, state, and federal resources when it is needed. (Part of the Newcomers to America series; available in eight languages.)

Newcomers to America, PO Box 339, Portland, OR 92707

P: 800-776-1610; F: 503-241-3507

Displaced in the New South

1995; 57 mins.; VHS

This case study explores the cultural clash between Latino and Asian immigrants in Georgia. The film provides a sensitive study of the influx of large numbers of culturally different immigrants who have settled in the suburbs and urban centers of the U.S.

Center for Media and Independent Learning, 2000 Center Street, 4th Floor, Berkeley, CA 94704

P: 510-642-0460; F: 510-643-9271; e-mail: cmil@uclink.berkeley.edu

Do Two Halves Really Make a Whole?

1993; 30 mins.; VHS

This video shows the points of view of people of multiracial Asian heritages and how they live their lives with the influences of the differing cultures.

NAATA Distribution, 346 Ninth Street, 2nd Floor, San Francisco, CA 94103

P: 415-552-9550; F: 415-863-7428; e-mail: naata@sirius.com

Doing Business in Asia

1989; 60 mins. each; VHS

> This four-part series covers the cultural and psychological factors involved in U.S./Asian business relationships: *Doing Business in Korea, Doing Business in Taiwan, Doing Business in Hong Kong,* and *Doing Business in Japan.* They describe each nation and its heritage, how to avoid mistakes and understand each country's values and culture, how to build relationships, and other issues for foreign visitors and residents.
>
> Big World Inc., 4204 Tamarack Court, Suite 100, Boulder, CO 80304
> P: 800-682-1261; F: 303-444-6190; e-mail: bigworld@aol.com

Doing Business in Latin America

1994, 1996; 35-45 mins. each; VHS

> This series of four videos on Argentina (1996), Brazil (1996), Chile (1996), and Mexico (1994) takes the viewer into the heart of the business communities of each country. In addition to understanding the fundamentals of the economy and business culture, the basic dos and taboos are addressed. The communication skills are relevant to all who plan to spend time in one or all of these countries.
>
> Big World Inc., 4204 Tamarack Court, Suite 100, Boulder, CO 80304
> P: 800-682-1261; F: 303-444-6190; e-mail: bigworld@aol.com

Doing Business in Southeast Asia

1997; 45 mins. each; VHS

> This set comprises three videos: *Doing Business in Singapore, Doing Business in Malaysia,* and *Doing Business in Indonesia.* Each video teaches how history gives context for the present-day business environment, how etiquette and culture can ensure a successful deal, and that relationships are critical to building alliances. The values of other cultures and communication techniques are described.
>
> Big World Inc., 4204 Tamarack Court, Suite 100, Boulder, CO 80304
> P: 800-682-1261; F: 303-444-6190; e-mail: bigworld@aol.com

Doing Business in Vietnam

1996; 30 mins.; VHS

> This program unfolds Vietnam's unique business culture, customs, and people. It presents many pointers from business leaders in Vietnam, including key legal considerations and dangerous pitfalls.
>
> Big World Inc., 4204 Tamarack Court, Suite 100, Boulder, CO 80304
> P: 800-682-1261; F: 303-444-6190; e-mail: bigworld@aol.com

Dormitory Diversity: Developing Cultural Awareness and Language Skills

1994; 30 mins.; VHS

The key to resolving dormitory conflicts between American and international students is mutual respect. With a focus on student dynamics, this video outlines tools for effective communication and awareness when cultures collide. It was made by the George Mason University English Language Institute.

NAFSA Publications, PO Box 1020, Sewickley, PA 15143

P: 800-836-4994; F: 412-741-0609; e-mail: inbox@nafsa.org

Doubles: Japan and America's Intercultural Children

1995; 84 mins.; VHS

This program is the first in-depth look at the lives of the intercultural children of Japanese and Americans from inside America as well as from inside Japan. Featuring persons from the turn of the twentieth century onward, it shows the nuances of cultural blending and ethnicity, what has changed, and what has remained the same from post-World War II until today. There is a shorter 55-minute version as well as a 22-minute derivative version, titled *A Culture in Common,* for K-12 audiences.

Doubles Film Library, 22-D Hollywood Avenue, Hohokus, NJ 07423

P: 800-343-5540; F: 201-652-1973

Dull Guys, The

1986; 30 mins.; VHS

This video is designed to sensitize service units on and off campus as well as international students to cultural stereotyping and language—induced miscommunications that occur within the university community. Nationality groups featured are Indonesians, Chinese, Latin Americans, and Arabs.

NAFSA Publications, PO Box 1020, Sewickley, PA 15143

P: 800-836-4994; F: 412-741-0609; e-mail: inbox@nafsa.org

Emerging Leaders

1991; 21 mins.; VHS

The emergence of disabled persons as leaders in the world community and the leadership skills gained through international educational exchange are discussed. The video features participants in Mobility International USA's leadership exchanges from Mexico, Australia, Malaysia, Zambia, and the U.S., including leadership specialists and disability activists. The message is one of empowerment and the importance of international leadership movements. (Also available in captioned and Spanish versions.)

Mobility International USA, PO Box 10767, Eugene, OR 97440

P: 541-343-1284

English as a Second Language
1973; 66 mins.; VHS

Three films, each twenty-two minutes, provide the following: Part I, *Introductory Grammar*; Part II, *Introductory Composition*; Part III, *Advanced Pronunciation*. (Currently available on ³/₄ U-matic format, but can be transferred to VHS on request.)

UCLA Instructional Media Library, 46 Powell Library, Los Angeles, CA 90095

P: 310-825-0755; F: 310-206-5392; e-mail: imlib@ucla.edu

Ethnic Notions
1987; 56 mins.; VHS

The viewer is taken on a disturbing voyage through American history and culture, examining racial stereotypes in detail and interweaving minstrel shows, greeting cards, advertisements, popular songs, cartoons, films, and household artifacts to link each stereotype to white society's shifting need to justify black oppression.

California Newsreel, 149 Ninth Street, San Francisco, CA 94103

P: 415-621-6196; F: 415-621-6522; e-mail: newsreel@ix.netcom.com

EuropeBOUND
1995; 25 mins. each; VHS

This three-part series provides practical information for students planning to travel independently to Europe. *On Your Own* covers planning for a trip to Europe as well as many of the day-to-day concerns that travelers may have: handling money matters, dealing with post offices, and meeting Europeans. *Hitting the Rails* portrays rail travel via the compartments, wagons, and train stations. *Turning In and Eating Out* introduces travelers to the basics of low-cost accommodations and restaurants.

Council on International Educational Exchange (CIEE), Information and Student Services Dept., 205 E. 42nd Street, New York, NY 10017

P: 212-822-2600; F: 212-822-2699

F-1 Student Visas and Status in the U.S.
1995; 75 mins.; VHS

Working through the maze of student regulations, the following topics are presented: inspection and arrival in the U.S., duration of status, change to student status while in the U.S., extension of stay, reinstatement to student status, reduced course load, transfer of schools, visa revalidation, dependents, employment, practical training, economic hardship employment, and internships.

Immigration Educational Services, 6300 Wilshire Boulevard, Suite 1010, Los Angeles, CA 90048

P: 800-705-5544; F: 213-966-4980

Families

1988; 15 mins. each; VHS

This series of five films depicts cross-cultural scenes of life among Japanese, American, and Maya Indian families. The same three families appear in all five films, titled *Alike and Different*, *Earning and Spending*, *Food and Eating*, *Helping Out*, and *Teaching and Learning*. The series is aimed at primary-level education.
Churchill Films, 6677 N. Northwest Highway, Chicago, IL 60631
P: 800-334-7830; F: 773-775-5091

Family across the Sea

1991; 56 mins.; VHS

Roots is retold as an historical and linguistic detective story. It shows how scholars have uncovered amazing examples of cultural retention between the Gullah people of South Carolina's Sea Islands and the people of the West African nation of Sierra Leone. It includes the moving return of a Gullah delegation to Sierra Leone and the African family they hadn't realized they had.
California Newsreel, 148 Ninth Street, #420, San Francisco, CA 94103
P: 415-621-6196; F: 415-621-6522; e-mail: newsreel@ix.netcom.com

Family Law in America

1989; 13 mins.; VHS

Many newcomers are from societies where the male head of the household controls the lives of those in his family. This program introduces a Southeast Asian family that learns about American domestic law under difficult, but common, circumstances. (Part of Newcomers to America series; available in fifteen languages.)
Newcomers to America, PO Box 339, Portland, OR 97207
P: 800-776-1610; F: 503-241-3507

Farewell to Freedom

1981; 55 mins.; VHS

Told in the context of America's contemporary immigration problems, this is the story of the struggle of the Hmong people of Laos, staunch allies of the U.S. during the Indochina War, to escape persecution. Hmong who have managed to emigrate to America face cultural problems and unemployment.
Instructional Support Services, Indiana University, Bloomington, IN 47401
P: 812-855-2103; F: 812-855-8404; e-mail: issmedia@indiana.edu

Favourable Exchange: International Students in Canada

1988; 30 mins.; 16 mm; VHS

This video explains the rewards and obstacles for young people who come to Canada for their education. It examines what these students leave behind, as well as the benefits their presence brings. Four students are profiled, all with unique experiences and facing unique challenges. It is useful as an orientation tool and as sensitization for institutional staff and host communities.

Canadian Bureau for International Education, 220 Laurier Avenue W., Suite 1100, Ottawa, ON K1P 5Z9 Canada

P: 613-237-4820; F: 613-237-1073

Finding a Job in America

1996; 12 mins.; VHS

The sheer volume and variety of industries in the U.S. is staggering to most newcomers. This program shows, through several examples, effective ways to increase the prospect of landing employment through techniques of self-assessment, job search, and applying for work. It also explores ways to identify and endure feelings of rejection and disappointment. (Part of the Newcomers to America series; available in eight languages.)

Newcomers to America, PO Box 339, Portland, OR 92707

P: 800-776-1610; F: 503-241-3507

Fishing, Hunting, and Firearms

1989; 10 mins.; VHS

This program deals with hunting and fishing regulations and firearm safety. It explains conservation as the motive for regulating these activities, as well as the proper ways to go about safe sporting procedures. (Part of the Newcomers to America series; available in fifteen languages.)

Newcomers to America, PO Box 339, Portland, OR 97207

P: 800-776-1610; F: 503-241-3507

Fishing in the City

1991; 28 mins.; VHS

This documentary explores the fishing habits and customs of various ethnic groups in Washington, D.C., the social bonds of these groups, and activities that help build bridges between them.

Center for Media and Independent Living, 2000 Center Street, 4th Floor, Berkeley, CA 94704

P: 510-642-0460; F: 510-643-9271; e-mail: cmil@uclink.berkeley.edu

Follow Me to America

1991; 30 mins. each; VHS

Each of the thirty course units, designed for Spanish-speaking adult learners, features a related group of language forms at progressively more advanced levels. Ten thematic areas—ranging from identifying people, places, and things to discussing likes and dislikes—are treated throughout the course so that students can build on their knowledge and put it to practical use. Comedy sketches, thrillers, and short documentaries are used in the eight tapes.

Audio-Forum, 96 Broad Street, Suite ES9, Guilford, CT 06437

P: 800-243-1234; F: 888-453-4329; e-mail: info@audioforum.com

Follow Me to San Francisco

1980; 60 mins.; VHS

This multimedia course is designed to give students insight into the verbal and nonverbal aspects of American English, as well as to develop their language skills. Presented in soap opera format, it depicts the adventures of Tom Williams, an eighteen-year-old man from Indiana, during his first visit to San Francisco. The situations, such as finding a job and an apartment, are similar to those of people new to the U.S.

Audio-Forum, 96 Broad Street, Suite ES9, Guilford, CT 06437

P: 800-243-1234; F: 888-453-4329; e-mail: info@audioforum.com

Food—A Cross-Cultural Study, Parts 1 and 2

1990; 38 mins.; VHS

This production covers food substance, preparation, and customs. It discusses how people obtain and eat food, from hunting-gathering to advanced agriculture and food distribution. Food and famine in the world today are examined.

Educational Design, 245 Hudson Street, New York, NY 10014

P: 800-221-9372; F: 212-675-6992

For Our Bread

1990; 26 mins.; VHS

Western influences, no matter how well intentioned, can erode the cultural identity of the people of developing nations. Interviews with native Malians reveal that the language, religion, and ideology of donor nations are often infused into and even dominate indigenous ethnic and regional practices.

Instructional Support Services, Indiana University, Bloomington, IN 47401

P: 812-855-2103; F: 812-855-8404; e-mail: issmedia@indiana.edu

Foreign Student Advising 101

1989; 33 mins.; VHS

Via three vignettes, this video, in a TV panel show format and a series of sketches, conveys information about foreign student advising and provokes thought about some of the issues that arise in a foreign student adviser's work. With an accompanying manual, it is intended for use in workshops or other group situations, but is also useful to individuals.

NAFSA Publications, PO Box 1020, Sewickley, PA 15143

P: 800-836-4994; F: 412-741-0609; e-mail: inbox@nafsa.org

Foreign Talk

1993; 11 mins.; VHS

When a Chinese American woman and two African American men make contact on a commuter train, cultural tensions are evident in their verbal exchange. Eventually the drama gives us possibilities for human relationships. There is good discussion material for cross-cultural communication and stereotypes.

NAATA Distribution, 346 Ninth Street, 2nd Floor, San Francisco, CA 94103

P: 415-552-9550; 415-863-7428; e-mail: naata@sirius.com

Four Families

1959; 60 mins.; 16 mm.

This film by noted anthropologist Margaret Mead provides an on-the-spot comparison of family life in India, France, Japan, and Canada, through the upbringing of a one-year-old child in a rural setting. It shows how child care—dress, bathing, feeding, and discipline—is related to national character. Though dated, this production is a timeless study of enculturation.

Center for Media and Independent Learning, 2000 Center Street, 4th Floor, Berkeley, CA 94704

P: 510-642-0460; F: 510-643-9271; e-mail: cmil@uclink.berkeley.edu

Freckled Rice

1983; 48 mins.; 16 mm; VHS

Thirteen-year-old Joe Soo is an American-born Chinese living in a world where adults speak Chinese and his friends speak English—a situation ripe with cultural conflicts and misunderstanding. With humor and poignancy, Joe, who lives in Boston's Chinatown, searches for his cultural identity.

Third World Newsreel, 335 West 38th Street, New York, NY 10018

P: 212-947-9277; F: 212-594-6417; e-mail: twn@twn.org

From Freak Street to Goa

1988; 60 mins.; VHS

While many Western idealists of the 1960s migrated to the East, most eventually returned home. This film chronicles the lives of four who chose to remain in India and Nepal, maintaining themselves in the foreign culture by becoming entrepreneurs.

Filmakers Library, Inc., 124 East 40th Street, New York, NY 10016

P: 212-808-4980; F: 212-808-4983; e-mail: info@filmakers.com

From Here, From This Side

1988; 24 mins.; VHS

Using mostly stock footage, this collage-like documentary "stars" Robert Redford, John Gavin, and Superman in an exploration of the largest border separating the First and the Third World—that separating the U.S. and Mexico. With texts by Octavio Paz and others and images from Mexican melodramas and Hollywood movies, this video forces Americans to consider cultural imperialism from the other side.

Women Make Movies, 462 Broadway, 5th Floor, New York, NY 10013

P: 212-925-0606; F: 212-925-2052

From Oh, No to OK: Communicating with Your International Teaching Assistant

1994; 10 mins.; VHS

Consisting primarily of short vignettes, this program is designed to be used to assist U.S. undergraduates in establishing productive communication patterns with their international teaching assistants. A facilitator's guide is included.

Michigan State University, Division of Student Affairs and Services. Internationalizing Student Life, 101 Student Services Bldg., East Lansing, MI 48823-1113

P: 517-355-8288

From Survival to Adaptation: The Adolescent Refugee Experience

1988; 22 mins.; VHS

This program focuses on the refugee experience of five adolescents from El Salvador, Vietnam, Cambodia, Afghanistan, and Laos, who participated as panelists at a meeting sponsored by the International Counseling Center. It is an introduction to, or takeoff point for, training or educational programs for counselors, social workers, and others concerned with refugee mental health.

Media Sales, The Pennsylvania State University, 118 Wagner Bldg., University Park, PA 16802

P: 800-770-2111; F: 814-865-3172; e-mail: mediasales@cde.psu.edu

Gerónimo: His Story

1996; 28 mins.; VHS

This film shows what it is like to be an illegal alien. Gerónimo came to California, learned English, worked, and sent money home to Mexico. He seeks an American college education and plans to return to Mexico to help his community. A human face is placed on the border problems between the U.S. and Mexico.
Filmakers Library, Inc., 124 East 40th Street, New York, NY 10016
P: 212-808-4980; F: 212-808-4983; e-mail: info@filmakers.com

Global Groove

1973; 30 mins.; VHS

In this classic video collage, Nam June Paik demonstrates how video can be used as a nonverbal means of communication to promote international understanding. Charlotte Moorman and Alan Shulman perform a cello duet.
Electronic Arts Intermix, 536 Broadway, 9th Floor, New York, NY 10012
P: 212-337-0680; F: 212-337-0679; e-mail: info@eai.org

Global One: The Art and Science of Global Success

1999; 40 mins. each; VHS

This program is in three parts, *Cross-Cultural Understanding, Intercultural Communicating,* and *International Negotiating.* Each video is filmed on location and includes advice from business executives, recognized authors, and cross-cultural specialists.
Big World Inc., 4204 Tamarack Court, Suite 100, Boulder, CO 80304
P: 800-682-1261; F: 303-444-6190; e-mail: bigworld@aol.com

Globally Speaking: Skills and Strategies for Success in Asia

1997; 2¹/₂ hrs.; VHS

This three-part, six-video series focuses on building specific communication skills critical to the success of multinational organizations operating in Asia. It features scenarios of East-West interaction involving people from Hong Kong, Indonesia, Japan, Korea, Malaysia, Singapore, Taiwan, and Thailand. It shows common misunderstandings, how to select appropriate technology, and how to create an effective global communication strategy.
Meridian Resources Associates, 1741 Buchanan Street, San Francisco, CA 94115
P: 800-626-2047; F: 415-749-0124

Going International: Beyond Culture Shock

1983; 30 mins.; 16 mm; VHS

Experts explain the phases of the cross-cultural adjustment process for those moving abroad. Expatriate families describe their experiences and suggest strategies for overcoming culture shock. The needs of spouses and children during relocation are given particular attention.

Griggs Productions, 5616 Geary Boulevard, San Francisco, CA 94122

P: 800-210-4200, ext. 136; F: 415-668-6004; e-mail: griggs@griggs.com

Going International: Bridging the Culture Gap

1983; 30 mins.; 16 mm; VHS

The challenges of dealing with a foreign culture are examined. Incidents from around the world illustrate basic concepts of culture. Interviews with experts and foreign nationals show the importance of cross-cultural awareness and the impact of cultural differences.

Griggs Productions, 5616 Geary Boulevard, San Francisco, CA 94122

P: 800-210-4200, ext. 136; F: 415-668-6004; e-mail: griggs@griggs.com

Going International: Living in the U.S.A.

1986; 30 mins.; 16 mm; VHS

Foreigners face many challenges living in America. This film provides an overview of American society and culture, suggesting ways to deal with social relationships and advising on practical issues such as housing, banking, schools, and transportation.

Griggs Productions, 5616 Geary Boulevard, San Francisco, CA 94122

P: 800-210-4200, ext. 136; F: 415-668-6004; e-mail: griggs@griggs.com

Going International: Managing the Overseas Assignment

1983; 30 mins.; 16 mm; VHS

Communication problems in foreign situations are cited, with examples of U.S. travelers in India, Saudi Arabia, England, and Mexico, illustrating how cultural taboos and accepted standards of behavior differ around the world. We are shown how travelers can develop their communications skills and conduct to be more effective overseas.

Griggs Productions, 5616 Geary Boulevard, San Francisco, CA 94122

P: 800-210-4200, ext. 136; F: 415-668-6004; e-mail: griggs@griggs.com

Going International Safely

1987; 30 mins.; 16 mm; VHS

International travelers may be subject to risks, from terrorism to police arrest for violation of local criminal codes. This program emphasizes the relatively low risk of being subject to violence and the much higher risk of accidentally violating foreign laws. It also suggests ways to anticipate and prevent illness, accidents, and minor personal crimes.

Griggs Productions, 5616 Geary Boulevard, San Francisco, CA 94122

P: 800-210-4200, ext. 136; F: 415-668-6004; e-mail: griggs@griggs.com

Going International: Welcome Home Stranger

1983; 15 mins.; 16 mm; VHS

In encountering unexpected problems on returning home, family members share how they overcame the difficulties of "reentry" into the workplace, community, and school environments.

Griggs Productions, 5616 Geary Boulevard, San Francisco, CA 94122

P: 800-210-4200, ext. 136; F: 415-668-6004; e-mail: griggs@griggs.com

Going International: Working in the U.S.A.

1986; 30 mins.; 16 mm; VHS

The foreign-born are introduced to the realities of the American workplace via work scenes as well as interviews with foreign nationals. The program is designed to increase understanding of American work culture, to improve communication skills, and to reduce intercultural conflict.

Griggs Productions, 5616 Geary Boulevard, San Francisco, CA 94122

P: 800-210-4200, ext. 136; F: 415-668-6004; e-mail: griggs@griggs.com

Good Evening, Teacher

1987; 20 mins.; VHS

This video, produced by the Los Angeles Unified School District, presents an orientation for new teachers and an overview of a large adult E.S.L. program; its goals, the nature of the student body, sample lesson plans, and demonstration lessons.

Los Angeles Unified School District, KLCS, 1061 W. Temple Street, Los Angeles, CA 90012

P: 213-625-6958, ext. 8524 (Roy Rosell); F: 213-481-1019

Good Neighbors

1989; 11 mins.; VHS

In many other countries, the concepts of property, ownership, and privacy have developed differently than in the U.S. This program helps alleviate problems of assimilation into neighborhoods by discussing how to be a good neighbor—by American standards. (Part of the Newcomers to America series; available in fifteen languages.)

Newcomers to America, PO Box 339, Portland, OR 97207

P: 800-776-1610; F: 503-241-3507

Green Card: An American Romance

1982; 80 mins.; VHS

In this soap opera parody, which takes place in Southern California, a Japanese woman, Sumie Nobuhara, re-creates her real-life struggles to remain in America after losing her student visa. She becomes dependent on her husband and unhappy, losing sight of the independence she sought.

Electronic Arts Intermix, 536 Broadway, 9th Floor, New York, NY 10012

P: 212-944-4805; F: 212-941-6118; e-mail: eai@interport.net

Here to Help: The Police in America

1989; 21 mins.; VHS

This program explores the nature of the police in America as tax-supported civilian employees, created to defend the life, liberty, and property of every citizen. The program demonstrates that effective law enforcement in this country depends on the cooperation of its citizens. (Part of the Newcomers to America series; available in fifteen languages.)

Newcomers to America, PO Box 339, Portland, OR 97207

P: 800-776-1610; F: 503-241-3507

High School of American Dreams

1995; 30 mins.; VHS

International High School in New York enrolls recent immigrants from forty-three countries working together to learn a new language and to become familiar with their new society and with each other. Students learn to respect one another's differences. The school uses innovative teaching methods to facilitate communication and open discussion.

Filmakers Library, Inc., 124 East 40th Street, New York, NY 10016

P: 212-808-4980; F: 212-808-4983; e-mail: info@filmakers.com

Home Is in the Heart: Accommodating Persons with Disabilities into the Homestay

1991; 19 mins.; VHS

Combining practical advice and a "go for it" attitude, this video provides information and ideas on how to find a homestay and meet accessibility needs, along
with advice on accommodating other special needs of participants. Interviews
with homestay providers give suggestions and encouragement.

Mobility International USA, PO Box 10767, Eugene, OR 97440

P: 541-343-1284

Homecoming

1991; 20 mins.; 16 mm; VHS

This sensitive drama shows the clash of two cultures and the difficulty of finding
a balance in the process of assimilation. The young Jamaican American woman
returns home to the Bronx from her liberal arts college full of disdain for the
people in her family.

Third World Newsreel, 335 West 38th Street, 5th Floor, New York, NY 10018

P: 212-947-9277; F: 212-594-6417; e-mail: twn@twn.org

Horizons and Homelands: Integrating Cultural Roots

1995; 24 mins.; VHS

This program chronicles the lives of two families—a Native American family,
which has recently moved from a reservation to the city, and a family from Laos,
which recently immigrated to the same city. For each family integrating its culture, or even just retaining it, is a trying and difficult process. With honesty and
candor each explains cultural distinctions and how integration takes place in the
new environment.

Films for the Humanities and Sciences, PO Box 2093, Princeton, NJ, 08543-
2053

P: 800-257-5126; F: 609-275-3767

Hosting with AFS

1999; 15 mins.; VHS

The video begins with the emotion of departure day and goes back in time to the
experiences of three hosted students and their American host families. Shot in
the Midwest, the program also features volunteers who explain AFS's volunteer-
based support system.

AFS Intercultural Programs, Marketing Dept., 198 Madison Avenue, 8th Floor,
New York, NY 10016

P: 212-299-9000, ext. 340; F: 212-299-9090

Hot Water: Intercultural Issues Between Women and Men

1994; 25 mins.; VHS

Foreign students and U.S. study abroad students give candid impressions and realistic advice on adjusting to male-female relationships in the host culture. Stressing communication and respect, the video addresses public displays of affection, dating customs, gender stereotypes in the media, and homosexual relationships. U.S. legal implications and safety issues are discussed with experts.

NAFSA Publications, PO Box 1020, Sewickley, PA 15143

P: 800-836-4994; F: 412-741-0609; e-mail: inbox@nafsa.org

House of the Spirit

1984; 52 mins.; VHS

Cambodian refugees, whose culture was devastated by U.S. high-tech war and by Khmer Rouge genocide, try to restore a way of life in a new country. The focus is on how the Western health care system impacts on traditional health care practices of the Khmer and how resultant problems can be resolved.

American Friends Service Committee Video and Film Library, 2161 Massachusetts Avenue, Cambridge, MA 02140

P: 617-497-5273; e-mail: afscnero@igc.apc.org

Housing—A Cross-Cultural Study, Parts 1 and 2

1975/1990; 30 mins.; VHS

This updated program provides a worldwide survey of housing construction, population concentrations, and movements toward urbanization.

Educational Design, 245 Hudson Street, New York, NY 10014

P: 800-221-9372; F: 212-675-6922

How Beliefs and Values Define a Culture

1997; 24 mins.; VHS

The purpose of beliefs and values within a culture is examined. Art, music, history, and religion are just a few elements that assist in shaping cultural beliefs and values. An understanding of cultural values is explored through historical footage combined with contemporary images, and an explanation is offered of how modern technology is changing cultures around the world.

AGC/United Learning, PO Box 48718, Niles, IL 60714-0718

P: 800-424-0362; F: 847-647-0918; e-mail: bistern@interaccess.com

How Economic Activities Define a Culture
1997; 20 mins.; VHS

By exploring cultures as varied as Egypt and Norway, examples and key points are presented about a culture's economic activities through three primary types of production: service, industry, and agriculture. We learn how cultures use various economic systems to facilitate the trade of goods and services.
AGC/United Learning, PO Box 48718, Niles, IL 60714-0718
P: 800-424-0362; F: 847-647-0918; e-mail: bistern@interaccess.com

How Far Are You Willing to Go to Make a Difference?
1998; 15 mins.; VHS

This film shows the activities and the diversity of Peace Corps volunteers in different fields, such as health, business development, and education. Countries featured are Ecuador, Mongolia, South Africa, and Uzbekistan. (The video is most easily accessed, without charge, in any Blockbuster Video store nationwide.)
Peace Corps, 1111 20th Street, NW, Washington, DC 20526
P: 800-424-8580

How Geography Defines a Culture
1997; 18 mins.; VHS

The geographical elements of topography, climate, and natural resources influence the people of any culture. Definitions and examples range from people thriving high in the Himalayas to deep in the Australian outback.
AGC/United Learning, PO Box 48718, Niles, IL 60714-0718
P: 800-424-0362; F: 847-647-0918; e-mail: bistern@interaccess.com

How Social Organizations Define a Culture
1997; 22 mins.; VHS

This program explores the influences of various social organizations on members of a culture, through family, work, and religious and educational groups. It also deals with different governmental and political philosophies adopted by a culture. It shows how ethnic groups function in a culture, and, in the case of immigration, how they allow cultural members the ability to retain ties to their heritage while being assimilated.
AGC/United Learning, PO Box 48718, Niles, IL 60714-0718
P: 800-424-0362; F: 847-647-0918; e-mail: bistern@interaccess.com

How to Avoid Crime in America

1989; 16 mins.; VHS

This program teaches newcomers how to avoid becoming victims of crime by illustrating practical methods for protecting their homes, their property, and themselves. Securing and lighting your home, calling 911 when necessary, and knowing what to do if you are a victim of crime are some of the points touched upon. (Part of the Newcomers to America series; available in fifteen languages.)
Newcomers to America, PO Box 339; Portland, OR 97207
P: 800-776-1610; F: 503-241-3507

How to Welcome Business Visitors from Japan

1992; 33 mins.; VHS

This program focuses on the critical dos and don'ts of receiving Japanese visitors. It utilizes real-life dramatizations of U.S. businesspeople welcoming their counterparts from Japan.
Big World Inc., 4204 Tamarack Court, Suite 100, Boulder, CO 80304
P: 800-682-1261; F: 303-444-6190; e-mail: bigworld@aol.com

I Am Your Sister

1991; 60 mins.; VHS

In the fall of 1990, over 1,000 women, profeminist men, and youth from twenty-three countries gathered in Boston to forge global connections across cultural differences. The video makers recorded dozens of compelling and dynamic voices from Asia, Central America, and the Caribbean in this document of a vital international movement.
Third World Newsreel, 335 West 38th Street, 5th Floor, New York, NY 10018
P: 212-947-9277; F: 212-594-6417; e-mail: twn@twn.org

Images That Speak: The Cross-Cultural Communications Workshop

1991; 28 mins.; VHS

This program portrays a workshop that assists with promoting cross-cultural communication and understanding within an ethnically diverse classroom setting. Experiences and traditions of students from twelve different countries are shared. An instructional training manual is included.
Insight MCC, Inc., 507 Darwin Street, Santa Cruz, CA 95062
P: 831-458-1628; F: 408-458-2158; e-mail: quadrant@cruzio.com

In a Strange Land: Police and the Southeast Asian Refugee

1989; 19 mins.; VHS

This program is designed to help law enforcement officials work with refugees in the most appropriate and efficient manner, especially in times of stress. (Part of the Newcomers to America series; available in English only.)

Newcomers to America, PO Box 339, Portland, OR 97207

P: 800-776-1610; F: 503-241-3507

In America

30 mins. each; VHS

This home-study course in basic conversational English is based on subtitled segments of popular American films and TV programs. It comprises twenty 30-minute tapes in ten volumes.

International Resources K.K., Yamatane Ikebukuro Bldg., #5F, 1-11-22 Minami Ikebukuro, Toshima-ku, Tokyo 171, Japan

In English

1987; 60 mins. each; VHS

Each unit has four elements: a narrated tour of a well-known place in or near Los Angeles, the introduction of new vocabulary (visual dictionary), dialogue, and pronunciation. The presentation is on ten tapes and includes five workbooks.

Video Language Products, PO Box 641, South Pasadena, CA 91031-0641

P: 800-367-3806; F: 626-799-4729; e-mail: info@videolanguage.com

In English on Your Own

1989; 60 mins. each; VHS

In this series of lessons, accompanied by a workbook, on-screen instructors introduce the segments and demonstrate all the components and suggested oral exercises. The vocabulary and sentence structure are controlled to give the learner success at each level.

Video Language Products, PO Box 641, South Pasadena, CA 91031-0641

P: 800-367-4729; F: 626-799-4729; e-mail: info@videolanguage.com

In Our Classroom

1992; 28 mins.; VHS

This documentary shows a multicultural sixth-grade public school classroom in Los Angeles, where thirty-four children from fifteen different countries thrive and learn despite poverty, racism, and budget cuts. The film is especially significant for anyone interested in American education.

Center for Media and Independent Learning, 2000 Center Street, 4th Floor, Berkeley, CA 94704

P: 510-642-0460; F: 510-643-9271; e-mail: cmil@uclink.berkeley.edu

In Praise of Hands

1974; 28 mins.; 16 mm; VHS

Filmed in the Canadian Arctic, Finland, India, Nigeria, Japan, Mexico, and Poland, this program shows the special skills of artisans working at crafts which reflect the culture of their countries. Included are stone sculpture, pottery, ceramics, weaving, dyeing, puppet making and embroidery.

Canadian Film Distribution Center, SUNY Plattsburgh, Feinberg Library, Plattsburgh, NY 12901-2697

P: 800-388-6784; F: 518-564-2112

Inside America: Scenes of Everyday Life

1998; 200 mins.; VHS

This four-video and book program develops high-intermediate students' listening and speaking skills as well as their understanding of how to use English effectively within American culture. The units show real life in the U.S., not a Hollywood version. Scenes covered include applying for government services, voting in an election, using a computer, washing the car, visiting historic landmarks, baking a Thanksgiving turkey, shopping, and conducting a job interview.

Highland Publishing, PO Box 554, Los Gatos, CA 95031-0554

P: 408-353-5756; F: 408-353-3388; e-mail: esl@highlandpublishing.com

International Assignment

1992; 30 mins.; VHS

This film discusses problems faced by Americans assigned to posts in developing countries, such as language barriers, unfamiliar currency, restrictive mores, and resettling families. It also describes how the company's role can be expanded to assist overseas placement. Nigeria and New Zealand are used as country case studies.

Pennsylvania State University, Media Sales, 118 Wagner Building, University Park, PA 16802

P: 800-770-2111; F: 814-865-3172; e-mail: mediasales@cde.psu.edu

International Business Practices

1997; 40 mins.; VHS

Renowned anthropologist Edward T. Hall explores the hidden dimensions that have a profound influence on cross-cultural business relations: space, time, and the exchange of information. He explains American assumptions that lead to

troubling international and cross-cultural interactions, using footage from cultur-
ally diverse settings.
Intercultural Resource Corporation, 78 Greylock Road, Newtonville, MA 02460
P: 617-965-8651; F: 617-969-7347; e-mail: info@irc-international.com

Introduction to American Law

1989; 10 mins.; VHS

Some newcomers have a limited understanding of life in a constitutional repub-
lic. This program acquaints them with voting, the role of government, and some
of the individual rights guaranteed by our Constitution. (Part of the Newcomers
to America series; available in fifteen languages.)
Newcomers to America, PO Box 339, Portland, OR 97207
P: 800-776-1610 F: 503-241-3507

Introduction to American Public Schools

1989; 20 mins.; VHS

This program describes the legal requirements and social characteristics of the
American school system. It responds to schooling issues from grammar school
to high school and explains not only the role of education in America, but its
importance to young newcomers and their parents. (Part of the Newcomers to
America series; available in fifteen languages.)
Newcomers to America, PO Box 339, Portland, OR 97207
P: 800-776-1610; F: 503-241-3507

Introduction to the Arab World

1989; 48 mins.; VHS

This cross-culturally oriented presentation lays a foundation for exploring the
diversity and unity, cultural traditions, and contemporary concerns of the Arab
world. It is divided into three segments and is accompanied by a free comprehensive program guidebook.
AMIDEAST, 1730 M Street, NW, Suite 1100, Washington, DC 20036
P: 202-776-9600; F: 202-822-6563; e-mail: inquiries@amideast.org

Invisible Walls

1969; 12 mins.; VHS

This film focuses on common American beliefs about personal space, showing
that people encase themselves in invisible walls about eighteen inches from their
bodies and that violation of these imaginary walls causes a feeling of discomfort.
Center for Media and Independent Learning, 2000 Center Street, 4th Floor, Berkeley, CA 94704
P: 510-642-0460; F: 510-643-9271; e-mail: emil@uclink.berkeley.edu

Islam and Christianity

1993; 30 mins.; VHS

This program examines the historical relations between Islam and Christianity and the long history of conflict between them. Iran's ambassador to the Vatican, Mohammed Masjed Jame'i, explains the basic differences and similarities between Islam and Christianity, the roles of Christ and Muhammed, the Bible and the Koran, and the main differences in approach.

Films for the Humanities and Sciences, PO Box 2053, Princeton, NJ 08543-2053
P: 800-257-5126; F: 609-275-3767; e-mail: custserv@films.com

Islam and Pluralism

1993; 30 mins.; VHS

Anwar Ibrahim, Malaysia's controversial Minister of Finance and Deputy Prime Minister, explains his government's approach to multiculturalism within Islam. Although Malaysia is a multicultural and multireligious society, the official religion is Islam.

Films for the Humanities and Sciences, PO Box 2053, Princeton, NJ 08543-2053
P: 800-257-5126; F: 609-275-3767; e-mail: custserv@films.com

Japan Bashing

1993; 22 mins.; VHS

Dominance by the Japanese in industry and commerce has served to inflame an historical prejudice against all Asians. From the anti-Chinese legislation of the late 1880s to the Japanese American citizens who were interned during World War II to the boycotts facing Korean shopkeepers, America has a tradition of bias against and fear of Asians. This overview of racism and prejudice was produced by WCBS-TV.

Carousel Film and Video, 260 Fifth Avenue, Suite 905, New York, NY 10001
P: 212-683-1660; F: 212-683-1662; e-mail: carousel@pipeline.com

Japanese American Women: A Sense of Place

1992; 28 mins.; VHS

The stereotype of the polite, docile, exotic Asian woman is shattered in this documentary, in which a dozen women speak about their experiences as part of the "model minority." It ultimately becomes the story of Japanese American women and their search for a sense of place.

Women Make Movies, 462 Broadway, 5th Floor, New York, NY 10013
P: 212-925-0606; F: 212-925-2052

Japanese Version, The
1991; 56 mins.; VHS

This video examines Western influences on contemporary Japanese culture and the way the Japanese have adapted foreign things to their own needs and culture. An earlier version was titled *America through Japanese Eyes*.

Distributor: Transit Media, 22D Hollywood Avenue, Hoho Kus, NJ 07423

Jennifer's Chinese Diary
1990; 28 mins.; VHS

Jennifer Lui is a typical 14-year-old living in New York City. She is half Chinese and half American. Self-questioning about her identity takes on a new dimension when her father asks her to join him in China. The ancient and modern world of China is revealed through Jennifer's diary as she grapples to understand the culture around her.

Carousel Film and Video, 260 Fifth Avenue, New York, NY 10001
P: 212-683-1660; F: 212-683-1662; e-mail: carousel@pipeline.com

Jew in the Lotus, The
1998; 60 mins.; 16 mm

In 1990 eight Jewish delegates traveled to Dharamsala, India, to meet with the Dalai Lama of Tibet and share the Jewish "secret of spiritual survival in exile." Included are images of the Tibetan enclave and interviews with progressive Jewish thinkers of North America as well as with the Dalai Lama himself.

Blind Dog Films, PO Box 238, Waban, MA 02168
P: 617-965-0712; F: 617-965-0384; e-mail: zauf@aol.com

Job Search, The: A Cultural Orientation
1988; 25 mins.; VHS

Skits and interviews are provided to assist refugees and immigrants in finding jobs in the U.S., through five 5-minute sections. A manual is included.

Jewish Vocational Service, Refugee Program, 105 Chauncy Street, 3rd Floor, Boston, MA 02111
P: 617-426-6990

Journeys: AFS Adventures in Latin America
1991; 13 mins.; VHS

Three U.S. teenagers travel to Latin America as AFS exchange students. We share in their growing self-confidence as they make new friends, develop family relationships, and embark on a variety of learning adventures.

AFS Intercultural Programs, Marketing Dept., 198 Madison Avenue, 8th Floor, New York, NY 10016
P: 212-299-9000, ext. 340; F: 212-299-9090

Knowing Her Place

1990; 40 mins.; VHS

Here is a moving investigation of the cultural schizophrenia experienced by Vasu, an Indian woman who has spent most of her life in the U.S. Vasu's relationships with her mother and grandmother in India and with her husband and teenage sons in New York reveal profound conflicts between her traditional upbringing and her personal and professional aspirations.

Women Make Movies, 462 Broadway, 5th Floor, New York, NY 10013
P: 212-925-0606; F: 212-925-2052

Korea: Homes Apart

1991; 55 mins.; VHS

Producer/narrator Christine Choy travels to South Korea to find her own heritage and simultaneously traces the journey of a Korean American to find his lost sister in North Korea. This was the first independent film crew permitted to film in both North and South Korea. In addition to providing cross-cultural insights, it shows the pain of families separated by the division of Korea into two hostile countries.

Third World Newsreel, 335 West 38th Street, 5th Floor, New York, NY 10018
P: 212-947-9277; F: 212-594-6417; e-mail: twn@twn.org

Kuro-Kuro: A Portrait of Ethnocentrism and Cultural Relativity

1982; 14 mins.; VHS

Set within the context of a talk show on Philippine television, this film stresses the role of sociological perspectives in understanding cultural relativity and ethnocentrism. Two college-age women from another culture discuss American society in a classically ethnocentric way. Issues discussed focus upon the immediate social environment as it relates to family, sex roles, life cycle, and human values.

Iowa State University Media Resources Center, 121 Pearson Hall, Ames, IA 50011
P: 515-294-1540

Language Teaching in Action: Videos for Teacher Training, #1—Grammar

1995; 20 mins.; VHS

This video features a communicative grammar lesson in a university E.S.L. classroom. The focus is the past perfect tense, and elements of the lesson include presentation of context, form and meaning, and focused practice. Cuts of the instructor describing what she is doing and why are featured throughout.

Patricia A. Porter, English Dept., San Francisco State University, 1600 Holloway Avenue, San Francisco, CA 94132
P: 415-338-1320; e-mail: pporter@sfsu.edu

Learning About Language

1985; 7 hrs.; VHS

The principles of language acquisition, how to differentiate specific language difficulties from overall adjustment issues, and how to assess and interpret language proficiency are featured in this unit. Part of the Intercultural Communication series. A language learning simulation is included.

Youth For Understanding Program Services, 3501 Newark Street, NW, Washington, DC, 20016

P: 800-424-3691, ext. 134; F: 202-895-1104

Learning English

1992; 2 hrs. each; VHS

Twenty units of four lessons per unit use real-life situations to teach E.S.L. Topics include: making friends, health care, marketing, buying clothing, on the job, buying a car, special occasions, money, emergencies, driving a car, the neighborhood, looking for housing, recreation and leisure, getting a job, fitness, apartment living, getting around the city, the telephone, schools, and government.

Delta Systems, 1400 Miller Parkway, McHenry, IL 60050-7030

P: 800-323-8270; F: 800-909-9901

Learning to Hate

1998; 39 mins.; VHS

Bill Moyers focuses on how children learn to hate and how attitudes toward hatred differ from culture to culture. A youth of Arab-Israeli descent becomes friends with an Orthodox Jew. High school students analyze the origins of hatred against gays. A Holocaust survivor teaches children how stereotyping breeds hatred. Experiences are shared by Jimmy Carter, Nelson Mandela, Elie Wiesel, Vaclav Havel, Li Lu, and Northern Ireland peace activist Mairead Corrigan Maguire.

Films for the Humanities and Sciences, PO Box 2093, Princeton, NJ 08543-2053

P: 800-257-5126; F: 609-275-3767

Leaving Bakul Bagan

1994; 45 mins.; VHS

This moving documentary shows a young Indian woman's desire for travel, education, and experience, and her conflict with family and national loyalties.

Third World Newsreel, 335 West 38th Street, 5th Floor, New York, NY 10018

P: 212-947-9277; F: 212-947-6417; e-mail: twn@twn.org

Leaving Home: The American Experience of Six International Students

1990; 40 mins.; VHS

In an interview setting, six international students express their needs and concerns upon entering the U.S. This video, which was produced by The School of the Art Institute of Chicago, provides insight into aesthetic perception and education in the arts from a cultural viewpoint. The students' comments have import for students, faculty, and staff in a variety of disciplines other than the arts.

NAFSA Publications, PO Box 1020, Sewickley, PA 15143

P: 800-836-4994; F: 412-741-0609; e-mail: inbox@nafsa.org

Letters Not about Love

1998; 58 mins.; 16 mm; VHS

Two poets, one from America, the other from Russia, are asked to begin a correspondence based on a list of ordinary words such as home, book, poverty, and violence. They reflect on each word, considering its conventional meaning and what it means to them personally. As the film progresses, both the similarities and differences between Russian and American ways of grasping the world are revealed, providing a compelling expression of mutual understanding.

New Day Films, 22-D Hollywood Avenue, Hohokus, NJ 07423

P: 201-652-6590; F: 201-652-1973; e-mail: tmcndy@aol.com

Little Street Wisdom, A

1989; 23 mins.; VHS

Targeted at new arrivals and international student orientation program audiences, this video introduces the students to life in U.S. cities, points out precautions to take for safety, and shows them how to behave if they become the victim of a crime. Content is summarized at the end with familiar pictures to enhance understanding and retention.

NAFSA Publications, PO Box 1020, Sewickley, PA 15143

P: 800-836-4994; F: 412-741-0609; e-mail: inbox@nafsa.org

Living in a Consumer Society

1989; 19 mins.; VHS

This program addresses several elements of consumerism that may pose problems for newcomers unfamiliar with buying and selling goods in America. Contracts and warranties, both verbal and written, are discussed, along with credit cards, checks, and the use of cash. The program explains how to protect yourself from fraudulent business practices and stresses personal responsibility for debts. (Part of the Newcomers to America series; available in fifteen languages.)

Newcomers to America, PO Box 339, Portland, OR 97207

P: 800-776-1610; F: 503-241-3507

Living in Africa: African Solutions to African Problems

1996; 30 mins. each; VHS

Three films, *Masai in the Modern World—Kenya, The Survival Age—Tanzania,* and *A Land of Immense Riches—Mozambique,* deal with the strains of modernization versus tradition, environmental issues, and the failures of past political systems.

Filmakers Library, Inc., 124 East 40th Street, New York, NY 10016
P: 212-808-4980; F: 212-808-4983; e-mail: info@filmakers.com

Looking Back, Looking Forward

1987; 22 mins.; VHS

This video promotes the important role that people with disabilities have in participating in international educational exchange and travel programs. People who are quadriplegic, blind, and deaf or who have cerebral palsy, along with nondisabled persons, discuss their experiences in England and Costa Rica. (Also available in captioned form for the hearing impaired.)

Mobility International USA, PO Box 10767, Eugene, OR 97440
P: 541-343-1284

Lost Secret 2000

1996; 100 mins.; VHS

This video consists of twenty episodes ranging from four to seven minutes each. It tells the story of an archeologist who loses, then regains his memory, a sinister professor and his beautiful assistant, and the long-lost secret of a vanished civilization in South and Central America. It is designed for elementary and low-intermediate E.S.L. students. The intriguing story helps retain high learning motivation.

Delta Systems, 1400 Miller Parkway, McHenry, IL 60050-7030
P: 800-323-8270; F: 800-909-9901

Maceo: Demon Drummer from East L.A.

1993; 44 mins.; VHS

The inspiring story of the life of a young Chicano musician depicts his fascination with Japanese Taiko drumming, which leads him to be invited to join the world-famous Ondekoza drummers. There is useful material here for cross-cultural discussion.

NAATA Distribution, 346 Ninth Street, 2nd Floor, San Francisco, CA 94103
P: 415-552-9550; F: 415-863-7428; e-mail: naata@sirius.com

Made in China

1987; 30 mins.; 16 mm; VHS

Lisa Hsia grew up typically American—her Chinese-born parents were completely assimilated. Her interest in things Chinese was limited to visiting Chinese restaurants. With verve and humor Lisa shares with us her voyage of discovery to China. Since she looks like a native but doesn't know how to behave like one, she initially gets in scrapes, but eventually discovers some truths about herself and her rich background.

Filmakers Library, Inc., 124 East 40th Street, New York, NY 10016

P: 212-808-4980; F: 212-808-4983; e-mail: info@filmakers.com

Mah-Jongg Orphan

1996; 45 mins.; VHS

This film depicts the cultural and generational chasm between a first generation Chinese immigrant and her American-born daughter. The universality of the issues transcends any particular race or culture.

Filmakers Library, Inc., 124 East 40th Street, New York, NY 10016

P: 212-808-4980; F: 212-808-4983; e-mail: info@filmakers.com

Mah-Jongg: The Tiles That Bind

1998; 27 mins.; VHS

Mah-jongg has been played in Asia since the time of Confucius. In the 1930s, Jewish women in immigrant neighborhoods quickly adopted this ancient Chinese game. The film provides a humorous glimpse of how two cultures, seemingly unrelated in America, converge.

btg productions, 26 Grove Street, #2E, New York, N Y 10014

P: 212-989-8978; F: 212-989-8978

Making the Most of It

1984; VHS

This 80-slide-and-tape program has been transferred to video. It takes newly arrived students through some of the experiences they will encounter during their first weeks in the U.K. and outlines what they will have to do to help themselves. (Produced by the British Council.)

Drake Educational Associates, St. Fagan's Road, Fairwater, Cardiff CF5 3AE, Wales

P: 44-1222-560333; F: 44-1222-554909

Mako

1979; 30 mins.; VHS

Mako is a veteran screen actor who, like other Asian American actors, has had to contend with Hollywood's stereotypic images of Asians. Through his eyes, the program examines these mass media images—from the early "screaming yellow hordes" cartoon depictions of the 1800s to the more current Kung Fu variety.

Educational Film Center, 5101-F Backlick Road, Annandale, VA 22003

P: 703-750-0560; F: 703-750-0566

Managing Daily and University Life in China

1989; 60 mins.; VHS

This documentary on preparing for and managing university life in China profiles U.S. Fulbright professors and their families. It is sponsored by the U.S. Fulbright Program and is produced by North State Public Video.

Dr. Pamela George, Professor of Educational Psychology, School of Education, North Carolina Central University, Durham, NC 27707

P: 919-560-5175; e-mail: pggeorge@nccu.edu

Managing Daily and University Life in Southeast Asia, Part I: Making It Manageable

1990; 48 mins.; VHS

This documentary on managing university life and work in Thailand, Malaysia, and Indonesia profiles U.S. Fulbright professors and their families. It is sponsored by the U.S. Fulbright Program and is produced by North State Public Video.

Dr. Pamela George, Professor of Educational Psychology, School of Education, North Carolina Central University, Durham, NC 27707

P: 919-560-5175; e-mail: pggeorge@nccu.edu

Managing Daily and University Life in Southeast Asia, Part II: Making It Meaningful

1990; 30 mins.; VHS

This documentary features the values of university life and work in Thailand, Malaysia, and Indonesia. U.S. Fulbright professors share the relevance of working across cultures to their professional work and their personal lives.

Dr. Pamela George, Professor of Educational Psychology, School of Education, North Carolina Central University, Durham, NC 27707

P: 919-560-5175; e-mail: pggeorge@nccu.edu

Managing in China
1998; 3 hrs.; VHS

This series of six videos addresses current best practices in key areas of management and human resources in China. The series offers practical advice from more than forty experienced managers and executives on how to address recruiting, training, localizing, managing performance, and transferring technology.

Meridian Resources Associates, 1741 Buchanan Street, San Francisco, CA 94115
P: 800-626-2047; F: 415-749-0124

Mi Casa Es Su Casa (Let My Home Be Your Home)
1986; 22 mins.; VHS

This video explores the lives of exchange participants from the U.S. and Costa Rica who volunteer to improve services to persons with disabilities, demonstrating the importance of persons both with and without disabilities volunteering in other countries.

Mobility International USA, PO Box 10767, Eugene, OR 97440
P: 541-343-1284

Microcultural Incidents in Ten Zoos
1971; 34 mins.; 16 mm; VHS

This film shows Professor Ray L. Birdwhistell demonstrating the context control method for comparative analysis of cross-cultural situations. Short film excerpts illustrate the interaction of family members with each other and with animals in zoos in England, France, Italy, Hong Kong, India, Japan, and the U.S. An epilogue illustrates observer and camera-operator biases in recording interactional data.

Pennsylvania State University Audio Visual Services, 17 Willard Bldg., University Park, PA 16802
P: 800-770-2111

Migrant's Heart, A
1996; 30 mins.; VHS

This video, produced by the BBC, examines life from the perspective of migrants as they strive to retain their cultural identities while adapting to the cultures of their adopted lands.

CPB Project, PO Box 2345, South Burlington, VT 05407-2345
P: 800-532-7637; F: 802-864-9846

Miles from the Border

1987; 15 mins.; 16 mm; VHS

Twenty years after emigrating from a rural village in Mexico to an ethnically divided community in California, the Aparicio family shares its experiences of dislocation and the difficulties of crossing cultures. Family members portray their struggles to learn English, to resist vocational tracking, to go on to universities, and to find balance in a multicultural society.

New Day Films, 22-D Hollywood Avenue, Hohokus, NJ 07423

P: 201-652-6590; F: 201-652-1973; e-mail: tmcndy@aol.com

Mr. Ahmed

1994; 52 mins.; 16 mm; VHS

This fictional drama of a young Indian expatriate living in a small town in America depicts his struggles to find a life for himself in a different culture. With constant memories of home and family in India, he comes to a critical turn which could destroy both his worlds.

Third World Newsreel, 335 W. 38th Street, 5th Floor, New York, NY 10018

P: 212-947-9277; F: 212-947-6417; e-mail: twn@twn.org

Misunderstanding China

1972; 51 mins.; 16 mm

This CBS news report examines sources of popular American attitudes and misunderstandings about China. It traces the history of contacts between Chinese and Americans and shows how pulp comics, posters, and especially films played an important role in forming racist attitudes and erroneous concepts in the U.S. about Chinese people and society.

Center for Media and Independent Learning, 2000 Center Street, 4th Floor, Berkeley, CA 94704

P: 510-642-0460; F: 510-643-9271; e-mail: cmil@uclink.berkeley.edu

Monterey's Boat People

1982; 29 mins.; VHS

This film closely examines the tension between the established Italian fishing community and the more recently arrived Vietnamese fishermen in California's Monterey Bay Peninsula. It documents a particular facet of anti-Asian sentiment and the conflicts faced by an industry that is itself fighting for survival.

NAATA Distribution, 346 Ninth Street, 2nd floor, San Francisco, CA 94103

P: 415-552-9550; F: 415-863-7428; e-mail: naata@sirius.com

Mosori Monika

1971; 20 mins.; 16 mm

A Spanish nun and an elderly Warao Indian woman work together in a remote village in Venezuela. The film shows how each woman uses the other one's culture to help ease the difficulties they encounter in village life.

Center for Media and Independent Learning, 2000 Center Street, 4th Floor, Berkeley, CA 94704

P: 510-642-0460; F: 510-643-9271; e-mail: cmil@uclink.berkeley.edu

Motor Vehicles and the Law

1989; 20 mins.; VHS

This video concentrates on motor vehicle laws, the requirements to operate a motor vehicle, and the operator's responsibilities. (Part of the Newcomers to America series; available in fifteen languages.)

Newcomers to America, PO Box 339, Portland, OR 97207

P: 800-776-1610; F: 503-241-3507

Mott to Mulberry

1992; 30 mins.; 16 mm; VHS

This lighthearted film features a second-generation Chinese American and his attraction to a local Italian girl. The situation results in a culture clash with his family as well as with the neighborhood.

Third World Newsreel, 335 West 38th Street, 5th Floor, New York, NY 10018

P: 212-947-9277; F: 212-947-6417; e-mail: twn@twn.org

Moving Mountains: The Story of the Yiu Mien

1990; 58 mins.; 16 mm; VHS

This film provides an intimate and caring look at the Yiu Mien, a group of Southeast Asian refugees who originally settled in the Pacific Northwest. In their native Laos, this hill tribe had no electricity, cars, or other twentieth century technology. Through rare archival footage of the Mien in their mountain homeland, their ancient culture is revealed. Complex realities of their struggle to adapt to American culture are portrayed.

Filmakers Library, Inc., 124 East 40th Street, New York, NY 10016

P: 212-808-4980; F: 212-808-4983; e-mail: info@filmakers.com

My America (or Honk If You Love Buddha)

1997; 87 mins.; 16 mm; VHS

Filmmaker Tajima-Peña traces the Asian American experience from her grandfather's settling in Los Angeles to present multicultural settings. She covers a variety of Asian American lives in urban and rural America as well as her own family's struggles through internment, immigration, and assimilation, including the civil rights movement and ongoing race relations dialogue.

Renee Tajima-Peña, PO Box 25692, Los Angeles, CA 90025

P: 310-479-2040; F: 310-477-2653; e-mail: tajimapena@aol.com

My Country Left Me

1995; 50 mins.; VHS

Because of repercussions stemming from the Arab-Israeli conflict, many Jews from Tunisia resettled in France. The specificity of the group's culture shock is explored. A pilgrimage back to Tunisia reveals the passionate identification three generations of Jews continue to feel for the country left behind.

Michkan World Productions, 25 rue Saint Sebastian, Paris 75011, France

P: 011-33-1-48 05 93 80; F: 011-33-1-48 05 06 63

Negotiating in Today's World

1993; 89 and 35 mins.; VHS

This two-video set features *Making Global Deals* and *Seven Principles of Negotiating*. Cultural, political, and ideological differences are identified, as well as overlooked details like jet lag.

Big World Inc., 4204 Tamarack Court, Suite 100, Boulder, CO 80304

P: 800-682-1261; F: 303-444-6190; e-mail: bigworld@aol.com

New Puritans, The: The Sikhs of Yuba City

1985; 27 mins.; VHS

Forced for economic reasons from their farms in the state of Punjab, the first Sikh immigrants came to California in the early 1900s, creating a rural life that mirrored their native India. This is a lucid portrait of the cultural and generational conflicts faced by all immigrant groups in the U.S.

NAATA Distribution, 346 Ninth Street, 2nd Floor, San Francisco, CA 94103

P: 415-552-9550; F: 415-863-7428; e-mail: naata@sirius.com

New Year
1987; 20 mins.; VHS

Soe, a fourth-generation Chinese American, uses coloring book characters to render her childhood ambivalence toward her heritage. She also uses clips from TV shows, movies, and comic books to confront the images which foster the kind of prejudice she experienced as a child. A hundred years of racist media messages about Asians are condensed into these tenacious stereotypes.

Women Make Movies, 462 Broadway, Suite 212, New York, NY 10013

P: 212-925-0606; F: 212-935-2052

Nirvana in Nova Scotia
1994; 25 mins.; VHS

The largest Buddhist community outside of Asia is in Halifax, Nova Scotia. This mostly American community has been an inspiration to the city. The film deals with the history of the community, why they settled there, and the culture shock they experienced.

Canadian Film Distribution Center, SUNY Plattsburgh, Feinberg Library, Plattsburgh, NY 12901-2697

P: 800-388-6784; F: 518-564-2112

Now You're Talking: English for Daily Living
1987; 80 mins.; VHS

Via ten 8-minute lessons, this video explores relationships between students, students and teachers, and students and friends. It includes a structural/functional syllabus.

Educational Activities, Inc., PO Box 392, Freeport, NY 11520

P: 516-223-4666; F: 516-623-9282; e-mail: learn@edact.com

Oasis of Peace
1995; 28 mins.; VHS

This is the story of the village of Neve Shalom/Wahat al-Salam, located in the heart of Israel. Here Jews and Palestinians, all Israeli citizens, have been living in harmony since 1978. In 1979 the residents established the School for Peace, which is the principal outreach institution of the community. The film documents the remarkable story of a village and its schools within the context of the Middle East conflict.

American Friends Service Committee Video and Film Library, 2161 Massachusetts Avenue, Cambridge, MA 02140

P: 617-497-5273; e-mail: afscnero@igc.apc.org

Oaxacalifornia

1995; 57 mins.; VHS

This documentary describes one transnational family as they travel back and forth between California and Mexico. The parents hold green cards and the children are U.S. citizens. The economic necessity of their living in two countries reveals the complex cultural mix that changes both societies and leaves the individuals between the two worlds.

Center for Media and Independent Learning, 2000 Center Street, 4th Floor, Berkeley, CA 94704

P: 510-642-0460; F: 510-643-9271; e-mail: cmil@uclink.berkeley.edu

Open Homes, Open Hearts: Hosting International Students

1987; 21 mins.; VHS

This video focuses on the recruitment, orientation, and training of American hosts for international students. It was developed to meet a need of community groups who work directly with hosts and international students. It presents the philosophy and benefits of hosting, the qualifications for hosts, some of the issues involved, and some practical suggestions for hosting.

NAFSA Publications, PO Box 1020, Sewickley, PA 15143

P: 800-836-4994; F: 412-741-0609; e-mail: inbox@nafsa.org

Other Side of Winter, The

1993; 16 mins.; VHS

Two international students serve as guides in this video about the cold winter months, teaching the importance of layering proper clothing, tips for navigating icy sidewalks and streets, and the way to convert temperature and windchill readings. It also addresses medical conditions that can occur in winter, including hypothermia, frostbite, and dry skin.

NAFSA Publications, PO Box 1020, Sewickley, PA 15143

P: 800-836-4994; F: 412-741-0609; e-mail: inbox@nafsa.org

Ourselves

1979; 30 mins.; VHS

Five Asian American women—a plumber, a dancer, a young woman, a college counselor, and a mother of five—are featured in direct-to-camera interviews. Each one shares her experience of growing up Asian and female in America, confronting Western standards of beauty, dating, and marriage, and learning the strength of self-acceptance.

Educational Film Center, 5101-F Backlick Road, Annandale, VA 22003

P: 703-750-0560; F: 703-750-0566

Outside the Classroom (or See Me during My Office Hours)

1988; 28 mins.; VHS

This video presents five vignettes of typical problems and situations faced by university teachers outside the classroom. It is best used as a vehicle for discussion in the training of new teaching assistants or anyone else beginning a career as a university teacher or lecturer.

Center for English as a Second Language, PO Box 210024, University of Arizona, Tucson, AZ 85721-0024

P: 520-621-7063; F: 520-621-9180

Pak Bueng on Fire

1987; 25 mins.; 16 mm; VHS

Here is a look into the struggle of Thai immigrants in Los Angeles: Ron, on a student visa, finds himself short of money for his tuition, while his friend Charlie, an illegal immigrant, works at a small grocery store in a depressed neighborhood. Ron takes a full-time (illegal) job. Dialogue is in English and Thai with English subtitles.

Visual Communications, 120 Judge John Aiso Street, Basement Level, Los Angeles, CA 90012

P: 213-680-4462; F: 213-687-4848

Palenque: Un Canto

1992; 48 mins.; VHS

The villagers of San Basilio de Palenque, Colombia, descendants of African rebel slaves, preserve and maintain the culture of their African forebears in their music, dance, and other aspects of their social lives. The film provides a documentation of their day-to-day struggles, in both their rural existence and their interaction with the neighboring city, displaying helpful insights about multicultural relations.

New Day Films, 22-D Hollywood Avenue, Hohokus, NJ 07423

P: 201-652-6590; F: 201-652-1973; e-mail: tmcndy@aol.com

Palm Play

1980; 30 mins.; 16 mm; VHS

This program explains the symbolism of why some cultures dance with palms open and some with palms covered. It demonstrates a cross-cultural method of relating dance style to cultures and social structures around the world.

Center for Media and Independent Learning, 2000 Center Street, 4th Floor, Berkeley, CA 94704

P: 510-642-0460; F: 510-643-9271; e-mail: cmil@uclink.berkeley.edu

Paul Pedersen: Developing Multicultural Awareness
1991; 105 mins.; VHS

This presentation is based on Pedersen's book *A Handbook for Developing Multicultural Awareness*. It details issues in multicultural counseling and therapy, covering multicultural assumptions, information, and action skills.

Microtraining Associates, Inc., PO Box 9641, Amherst, MA 01059-9641

P: 413-549-2630; F: 413-549-0212

Peering Up
1986; 20 mins.; VHS

This program is designed for those who are preparing orientation programs for international students. It explains the use of Canadian "buddies" in international student adjustment. It is accompanied by a manual.

Canadian Bureau for International Education, 220 Laurier Avenue W., Suite 1100, Ottawa, ON, K1P 5Z9 Canada

P: 613-237-4820; F: 613-237-1073

People and Culture
1989; 17 mins.; VHS

Viewers are introduced to first-generation Canadian immigrants from a variety of countries as well as descendants of Inuits and Native Americans. The program also includes a brief look at the "apartness" of the French Canadians in Quebec.

Encyclopaedia Britannica, 310 S. Michigan Avenue, Chicago, IL 60604

P: 800-554-9862; F: 312-294-2138

Perfect English Pronunciation
1991; 60 and 56 mins.; VHS

In Part One, *How to Pronounce Consonants,* the viewer will see how to form each sound, with clear direction, animation, and mouth close-ups. In Part Two, *How to Pronounce Vowels, Diphthongs, and Word Endings,* each sound is shown in an individual lesson and can be studied and reviewed as often as necessary.

Delta Systems, 1400 Miller Parkway, McHenry, IL 60050-7030

P: 800-323-8270; F: 800-909-9901

Phrase by Phrase Pronunciation Videotapes
1995; 4^1/2 hours; VHS

This set of five videotapes enhances listening comprehension and pronunciation skills by giving learners visual and auditory models. The sixteen lessons increase in complexity and recycle points of rhythm, stress, intonation, and the articulation of vowels and consonants.

Sunburst Media, PO Box 61885, Sunnyvale, CA 94088-1885

P: 408-245-8514; F: 408-245-8514; e-mail: sunburstm@aol.com

Planning for Study Abroad
1989; 25 mins.; VHS

This video presents the essential facts about study abroad. Information comes from students themselves, who help their peers think about opportunities—and issues—that international study presents. Guidance on academic credit and finances is offered by professional study abroad advisers.

Institute of International Education Books, 809 United Nations Plaza, New York, NY 10017

P: 800-445-0443; F: 301-206-9789; e-mail: iiebooks@pmds.com

Planting Seeds for Peace
1988; 23 mins.; VHS

This documentary promotes intercultural dialogue and understanding in the Middle East. Four teenagers—Israeli Arab, Jewish, and Palestinian—come together in the U.S. to share their cultures, discuss their personal lives, break down stereotypes, and present their perspectives on the Middle East conflict to American young people. An in-depth leader's guide is included.

The Video Project, 200 Estates Drive, Ben Lomond, CA 95005

P: 800-4-PLANET; F: 831-336-2168; e-mail: videoproject@videoproject.org

Price You Pay, The
1983; 29 mins.; VHS

This film provides a human look at the problems faced by Southeast Asian refugees newly arrived in the U.S. and their desperate hopes to create new lives for themselves and their children. It shows the potential discrepancy between America's creed of welcoming the homeless and how that creed is practiced.

NAATA Distribution, 346 Ninth Street, 2nd Floor, San Francisco, CA 94103

P: 415-552-9550; F: 415-863-7428; e-mail: naata@sirius.com

Professional Integration for a Smooth Passage Home
1986; 17 mins.; VHS

This USAID-funded production illustrates the steps a foreign student can take in preparing for home-country return to a professional role after U.S. study or training. It is recommended for workshops and counseling on the eve of return to the home country after study.

NAFSA Publications, PO Box 1020, Sewickley, PA 15143

P: 800-836-4994; F: 412-741-0609; e-mail: inbox@nafsa.org

Pronunciation Workout for Foreign Language Learners

1997; 33 mins.; VHS

This program introduces the concept of doing warm-up exercises for the vocal apparatus in preparation for speech production. It leads a group of students through a twenty-minute workout series including relaxation and the tensing and flexing of muscles. It ends with interviews of four students from different language backgrounds.

Sunburst Media, PO Box 61885, Sunnyvale, CA 94088-1885

P: 408-245-8514; F: 408-245-8514; e-mail: sunburstm@aol.com

Public Diplomacy

1996; 58 mins.; VHS

This program is divided into two sections: *Telling America's Story* and *The Road Ahead.* Featuring commentary from journalists David Gergen and John Chancellor, it chronicles America's recognition of its need to be understood abroad. It moves through the creation of the Voice of America and the U.S. Fulbright Program, the origin of the U.S. Information Agency, the end of the Cold War, and the advent of sophisticated communications technology. (Produced by the USIA Alumni Association.)

USIAAA, 3218 North Kenmore Street, Arlington, VA 22207

e-mail: patchat2@aol.com

Rainbow War

1986; 20 mins.; 16 mm; VHS

This film is an allegorical fairy tale that examines the concepts of ethnocentrism, fear of difference, and the potential for peaceful synergy between nations. It was nominated for an Academy Award as best live-action short subject.

Pyramid Film and Video, PO Box 1048, Santa Monica, CA 90406-1048

P: 800-421-2304; F: 310-453-9083; e-mail: info@pyramedia.com

Rassias in China

1991; 60 mins.; VHS

Professor John Rassias of Dartmouth College takes his unique methods for teaching languages to Beijing, where American and Chinese cultures meet in unexpected ways. The film explores profound questions about the process of encountering a second language and culture.

The Rassias Foundation, 6071 Wentworth Hall, Dartmouth College, Hanover, NH 03755

P: 603-646-2922

Real America, The: Scenes of Everyday Life
1997; 210 mins.; VHS

This E.S.L. training program contains units on practical aspects of American culture, services to the public in an American city, American government, growing up in America, working, leisure, and holidays throughout the year. Students will develop vocabulary, improve listening comprehension, and learn American proverbs while discussing issues relating to life in the U.S.

Highland Publishing, PO Box 554, Los Gatos, CA 95031-0554

P: 408-353-5756; F: 408-353-3388; e-mail: esl@highlandpublishing.com

Real Thing, The
1995; 225 mins.; VHS

This series of fifteen videotaped classes shows teacher-student interaction in a wide range of mainstream courses. It provides authentic examples of real classroom language and teaching skills vital to students' success at an American college or university. It is especially recommended for advanced E.S.L. students.

Highland Publishing, PO Box 554, Los Gatos, CA 95031-0554

P: 408-353-5756; F: 408-353-3388; e-mail: esl@highlandpublishing.com

Reassemblage
1982; 40 mins.; 16 mm; VHS

Filmed among diverse peoples in Senegal, this film challenges conventional ethnographic documentary approaches to non-Western cultures. It explores daily life and is rich in imagery, symbolism, and information, juxtaposing Western perceptions of these cultures with African perspectives. It enables audiences to look at the Third World anew and question their own cultural biases.

Third World Newsreel, 335 West 38th Street, 5th Floor, New York, NY 10018

P: 212-947-9277; F: 212-594-6417; e-mail: twn@twn.org

Refugee Women in America
1989; 13 mins.; VHS

When they first arrive in America, many refugee women are greeted with newfound freedom and equality. In some of their native countries, this type of independence for women is unusual. This program discusses the rights and opportunities women have in America, while being sensitive to difficulties that may arise when American ways clash with other cultures. (Part of Newcomers to America series; available in fifteen languages.)

Newcomers to America, PO Box 339, Portland, OR 97207

P: 800-776-1610; F: 503-241-3507

Refugee Youth in America

1989; 26 mins.; VHS

Difficulties that refugee youth commonly encounter in adapting to life in America are examined. Five young refugees share their experiences and discuss their coping skills: cultural and social adjustment, family relationships, language skills, education, and self-identity. (Part of the Newcomers to America series; available in fifteen languages.)

Newcomers to America, PO Box 339, Portland, OR 97207

P: 800-776-1610; F: 503-241-3507

Remembering Wei Yi-fang, Remember Myself

1995; 29 mins.; 16 mm; VHS

This film charts the influence of the six-year experience of an African American woman in Taiwan after college graduation. The filmmaker discovers, through another language and culture, how to be respected for what she is, without the constant of American racism, and how it helped her achieve self-knowledge.

Women Make Movies, 462 Broadway, 5th Floor, New York, NY 10013

P: 212-925-0606; F: 212-925-2052

Returning Home: A Program for Re-entry

1984; 45 mins.; VHS

This video is designed for those who are preparing international students to return from Canadian universities to their home countries. It is accompanied by a manual and questionnaire.

Canadian Bureau for International Education, 220 Laurier Avenue W., Suite 1100, Ottawa, ON K1P 5Z9, Canada

P: 613-237-4820; F: 613-237-1073

Sailing through English

1996; 65 mins.; VHS

This program uses the film, *The Dove*, as a primary text to build the E.S.L. student's listening comprehension and speaking skills. *The Dove* is based on the true story of Robin Lee Graham, a teenage boy who sailed around the world alone: his dream, the challenge, the struggle, the adventure, and even innocent romance. The video provides a thread to tie together lessons which focus on many language functions. Accompanying text and teacher's notes are available.

Delta Systems, 400 Miller Parkway, McHenry, IL 60050-7030

P: 800-323-8270; F: 800-909-9901

Search for Peking Dog

1995; 8½ mins.; VHS

This satire features a German wife trying to prepare the perfect meal for her Chinese husband. It promotes discussion of culture clash and gender roles.

NAATA Distribution, 346 Ninth Street, 2nd Floor, San Francisco, CA 94103

P: 415-552-9550; F: 415-863-7428; e-mail: naata@sirius.corn

Sing a Song Together

1990; 20 mins.; VHS

This is the story of PREP, a refugee camp program preparing six- to eleven-year-old Southeast Asian children for school in the U.S.

Center for Applied Linguistics, Refugee Service Center, 4646 40th Street, NW, Washington, DC 20016-1859.

P: 202-362-0700

Slaying the Dragon

1988; 60 mins.; VHS

America's image industries have not been kind to Asian American women. This film analyzes the roles and images of Asian women promulgated by Hollywood and network TV over the past decades. Film clips and interviews with actors and media critics trace the history of these stereotypes.

NAATA Distribution, 346 Ninth Street, 2nd Floor, San Francisco, CA 94103

P: 415-552-9550; F: 415-863-7428; e-mail: naata@sirius.com

So Far from India

1982; 49 mins.; 16 mm; VHS

Ashok, a young Indian immigrant, works at a New York City newsstand to earn enough money to bring his wife and son to the U.S. Once established, he enjoys his bachelor existence and postpones sending for them. Meanwhile, his despairing wife has lost face with Ashok's family on whom she depends. The tension mounts when Ashok journeys home to confront the situation.

Filmakers Library Inc., 124 East 40th Street, New York, NY 10019

P: 212-808-4980; F: 212-808-4983; e-mail: info@filmaker.com

So You Have a New Job

1996; 12 mins.; VHS

The first day on a new job can be a terrifying experience for newcomers, especially those who have limited English. This program addresses basic employee philosophies, ethics, and work habits, such as honesty, sincerity, punctuality, ap-

propriate attire and hygiene, and general rights and responsibilities of employ-
ment. (Part of the Newcomers to America series; available in fifteen languages.)
Newcomers to America, PO Box 339, Portland, OR 92707
P: 800-776-1610; F: 503-241-3507

Solutions to Culture Stress

1991; 240 mins.; VHS

Four one-hour lessons are designed to help a missionary enter and return home
enriched by a cross-cultural experience.
Emmaus Road International, 7150 Tanner Court, San Diego, CA 92111
P: 619-292-7020

Soviet Students Speak to America

1984; 20 mins.; VHS

Through a rare, close-up look at Soviet education, the film visits schools and
students in Leningrad (now St. Petersburg), Tbilisi, and Moscow, giving a sense
of the similarities and differences between the American and the former Soviet
school systems. It shows how much Russian students learn about America and
how little we know in comparison.
The Video Project, 200 Estates Drive, Ben Lomond, CA 95005
P: 800-4-PLANET; F: 831-336-2168

Speak to Me

1990; 55 mins. each; VHS

This program is available in Spanish, German, Korean, Mandarin, Russian, and
Vietnamese versions. Each volume has three 55-minute videos in English and a
student book with the lessons in both English and the learner's native language.
Designed primarily for self-instruction, it enables the learner to develop the abil-
ity to think in English through the natural association of words and actions shown
in real-life situations.
Audio-Forum, 96 Broad Street, Suite ES9, Guilford, CT 06437
P: 800-243-1234; F: 888-453-4329; e-mail: info@audioforum.com

Speaking American English at Work

1988; 60 mins.; VHS

On two 30-minute tapes we view a young Vietnamese refugee's experiences in
his search for a job in the U.S. A teacher's manual is included.
Audio-Forum, 96 Broad Street, Suite ES9, Guilford, CT 06437
P: 800-243-1234; F: 888-453-4329; e-mail: info@audioforum.com

Stage One: The Natural Approach to Speaking English
1986; 30 mins. each; VHS

Twelve 30-minute lessons provide mimes, skits, songs, drawings, and lessons to help students recognize the sounds and know the meanings of one thousand frequently used words.

Stage One Productions, 1457 S. Nutwood, Anaheim, CA 92804

P: 714-772-8707; e-mail: sissonva@aol.com

Step Style
1980; 30 mins.; 16 mm; VHS

This film offers an explanation of leg and foot movements in dance throughout the world, and how these movements relate to social structures, cultural patterns, work, and sports.

Center for Media and Independent Learning, 2000 Center Street, 4th floor, Berkeley, CA 94704

P: 510-642-0460; F: 510-643-9271; e-mail: cmil@uclink.berkeley.edu

Stereotypes
1990; 25 mins.; VHS

The first U.S.-Soviet animated coproduction is a witty parody of the superpowers' traditional views of one another. In the style of a TV game show, a cartoon rivalry escalates into a full-blown battle, then prophetically concludes with the melting of the wall these archrivals have built between them. It is the first collaborative film of its kind to celebrate the end of the Cold War.

The Video Project, 200 Estates Drive, Ben Lomond, CA 95005

P: 800-4-PLANET; F: 831-336-2168

Stereotyping (International Version)
1985; 4$^{1}/_{2}$ hrs.; VHS

This unit in the Intercultural Communication series focuses on defining and understanding stereotypes and considers the consequences of stereotyping for those who work with international populations. Exchange students from a number of different countries are shown.

Youth For Understanding Program Services, 3501 Newark Street, NW, Washington, DC 20016

P: 800-424-3691, ext. 134; F: 202-895-1104

Strategies for Educators: Teaching Hispanic Students
1987; 75 mins.; VHS

Designed to increase staff awareness of the special needs of minority students, this program presents appropriate teaching methods on five tapes: *Teaching His-*

panic Students: Establishing Connections; Limited English Students: Five Program Models; Limited English Students: Teaching in the Mainstream; Cooperative Learning: The Team Approach; and *Cooperative Learning: How It Works.*
Multicultural Media, Orange County Dept. of Education, 20 Kalmus Drive, Costa Mesa, CA 92628
P: 714-966-4341; F: 714-662-0983; e-mail: education-materials@ocde.k12.ca.us

Struggle and Success

1993; 85 mins.; VHS

Narrated by Ossie Davis, this program examines the complex lives of African Americans from all walks of life living in Japan. Despite the perception that Japanese view ethnic minorities as inferior, some African Americans have made Japan their home and profess to find Japanese culture more tolerant overall than American culture. A shorter 55-minute version, with study guide, is also available.
Doubles Film Library, 22-D Hollywood Avenue, Hohokus, NJ 07423
P: 800-343-5540; F: 201-652-1973

Study in Africa: New Opportunities for American Undergraduates

1997; 27 mins.; VHS

This video offers an overview of several U.S. study programs at a variety of African campuses. Interviews with African university faculty, administrators, and students, and with U.S. students studying there, answer a number of questions about the opportunities and benefits of studying at their institutions.
NCSA, African Studies Center, Michigan State University, 100 International Center, East Lansing, MI 48824-1035
P: 517-353-1700; F: 517-432-1209; e-mail: ncsa@pilot.msu.edu

Study in Canada

1984; 20 mins.; VHS

This is an introduction to Canadian postsecondary education for international students.
Canadian Bureau for International Education, 220 Laurier Avenue W., Suite 1100, Ottawa, ON, K1P 5Z9 Canada
P: 613-237-4820; F: 613-237-1073

Study in the U.S.: Engineering

1985; 28 mins.; VHS

How to prepare for careers in engineering and the various requirements to be met by foreign students at all degree levels in the U.S. are presented. The program includes what engineers do, characteristics of a good engineer, basic fields of engineering, and how to choose a field.

AMIDEAST, 1730 M Street, NW, Washington, DC 20036

P: 202-776-9600; F: 202-822-6563; e-mail: inquiries@amideast.org

Study in the U.S.: Graduate Medical Education

1990; 30 mins.; VHS

This program provides information about graduate medical education in the U.S. and the steps a foreign medical graduate must follow to qualify and apply for residency training. These include becoming certified by the Educational Commission for Foreign Medical Graduates, applying to residency programs, and enrolling in the National Residency Matching Program. The video also suggests some study and research alternatives to graduate medical training.

AMIDEAST, 1730 M Street, NW, Washington, DC 20036

P: 202-776-9600; F: 202-822-6563; e-mail: inquiries@amideast.org

Study in the U.S.: Humanities and Social Sciences

1986; 34 mins.; VHS

This video discusses the diversity of career possibilities in the humanities and social sciences, providing guidance on how to select a program, characteristics of study at undergraduate and graduate levels, and the application process and possibilities for financial assistance.

AMIDEAST, 1730 M Street, NW, Washington, DC 20036

P: 202-776-9600; F: 202-822-6563; e-mail: inquiries@amideast.org

Success Video Packages

1996; 30 mins. each; VHS

The program consists of four high-interest TV newsmagazines, including all the elements of a typical format such as cohosts, feature stories, commercials, and contests. The universal themes motivate E.S.L. students to improve their language skills as they find out more about the topics.

Addison Wesley Longman, 1 Jacob Way, Reading, MA 01867-3999

P: 800-358-4566; F: 781-944-9338

Success with English

1991; 45 mins. each; VHS

This program, a bilingual course for Spanish speakers, is one of the most extensive self-teaching video E.S.L. courses. It consists of 18 forty-five minute videos, 18 student workbooks, and 18 audiocassettes. It starts off with explanations in Spanish, which taper off as the student progresses.

Audio-Forum, 96 Broad Street, Suite ES9, Guilford, CT 06437

P: 800-243-1234; F: 888-543-4329; e-mail: info@audioforum.com

Talk to Me: Americans in Conversation
1996; 60 mins.; VHS

Americans from a variety of communities around the country are interviewed on the subject of what it means to be an American today. The program compares the relationship between personal and national history, culture, and politics; examines what unites and divides Americans as a people; and explores the role of race and ethnicity in the U.S. Included are interviews with numerous historians and writers from different cultural backgrounds.

The Cinema Guild, 1697 Broadway, Suite 506, New York, NY 10019-5904
P: 800-723-5522; F: 212-246-5525; e-mail: thecinemag@aol.com

Tanto Tiempo
1992; 26 mins.; 35 mm; VHS

This is the story of a young Mexican American woman and her Mexican mother who have adapted themselves to an Anglo lifestyle. Confronted with her past, the daughter rediscovers her Aztec ancestry and brings it back into her life.

Women Make Movies, 462 Broadway, 5th Floor, New York, NY 10013
P: 212-925-0606; F: 212-925-2052

Taxi-Vala/Autobiography
1996; 49 mins.; VHS

This film focuses on the lives and aspirations of South Asian immigrant taxi drivers in New York. It explores the complexity of the issues of the drivers and looks at the American dream within New York's South Asian communities.

Third World Newsreel, 335 W. 38th Street, 5th Floor, New York, NY 10018
P: 212-947-9277; F: 212-947-6417; e-mail: twn@twn.org

Teacher Training through Video: ESL Techniques
1988, 1989; 15 mins. each; VHS

This program begins skill-based training for E.S.L. teachers. In twelve tapes and interactive accompanying materials, the viewer is brought into a variety of classrooms in which a different language teaching technique is demonstrated. These techniques include lesson planning, focused listening, early production, dialogue, information gap, role play, problem solving, language experience, life skills reading, narrative reading, beginning literacy, and total physical response.

Addison Wesley Longman, 1 Jacob Way, Reading, MA 01867-3999
P: 800-358-4566; F: 781-944-9338

Teaching the Chinese Student

1989; 45 mins.; VHS

This documentary deals with effective techniques used by American Fulbright professors doing university teaching across cultures. It is sponsored by the U.S. Fulbright Program, and is produced by North State Public Video.

Dr. Pamela George, Professor of Educational Psychology, School of Education, North Carolina Central University, Durham, NC 27707

P: 919-560-5175; e-mail: pggeorge@nccu.edu

Techniques for Teachers: A Guide for Non-Native Speakers of English

1988; 110 mins.; VHS

Short segments from American university-level classes serve as language and behavior models to international teaching assistants.

University of Michigan Press, 830 Green Street, PO Box 1104, Ann Arbor, MI 48106-1104

P: 313-764-4392

Telling It Like It Is: Reflections on Cultural Diversity

1996; 62 mins.; VHS

An African American woman offers guidelines on how to deal with bigotry as she addresses racism, cultural identity, the power of words, postdiscrimination trauma, nonverbal communication, sexual orientation, and the power of healing.

Intercultural Resource Corporation, 78 Greylock Road, Newtonville, MA 02460

P: 617-965-8651; F: 617-969-7347; e-mail: info@irc-international.com

Terra Cognita's Live Abroad

1997; 30 mins.; VHS

This video is designed to provide new and soon-to-be expatriates with information about the expatriate experience. Life is presented through the eyes of families, couples, and individuals who have lived abroad, along with advice and explanations from experts in the field of international relocation.

Terra Cognita, 300 W. 49th St., Suite 314, New York, NY 10019

P: 212-262-4529; F: 212-262-5789; e-mail: terracognita@compuserve.com

Thanh's War

1991; 58 mins.; 16 mm; VHS

This is the story of a Vietnamese boy who at age twelve survived when his parents were killed in a grenade attack by American forces. Rescued and taken to the U.S., Thanh has made a successful life in the land he had considered his enemy. He grapples with the emotional legacy of the war, while trying to reconcile the two vastly different cultures within himself. He has traveled frequently to his ancestral village, where his traditional marriage is captured on film.

Center for Media and Independent Learning, 2000 Center Street, 4th Floor, Berkeley, CA 94704

P: 510-642-0460; F: 510-643-9271; e-mail: cmil@uclink.berkeley.edu

They Look at Your Face and See a Flag
1994; 20 mins.; PAL

Overseas students were interviewed within five months of their arrival in Britain, with the exception of one interviewed on the day of his departure. Their conversations deal with academic study, language, friends, diet, and general issues. This program is designed for use in orientation sessions.

Roselyn Cox, Sheffield University Television, University of Sheffield, Sheffield S10 2TN, England

P: 011-44-114-282-6063; F: 011-44-114-276-2306

To Canada: With Love and Some Misgivings
1992; 57 mins.; VHS

This video shows the concerns of the many ethnic groups living in Canada. The emerging viewpoint is one of respect, tolerance, and understanding for all cultures.

Canadian Film Distribution Center, SUNY Plattsburgh, Feinberg Library, Plattsburgh, NY 12901-2697

P: 800-388-6784; F: 518-564-2112

To Live in a Multicultural World
1994; 50 mins. each; VHS

This multimedia curriculum unit has nine lesson plans that address the consequences of stereotyping, illustrate ways to learn about other cultures, and help students to develop multiple cultural perspectives. It focuses on Mexican culture, while also offering examples of other cultural perspectives such as Japanese, Brazilian, and African American.

Youth For Understanding Program Services, 3501 Newark Street, NW, Washington, DC 20016

P: 800-424-3691, ext. 134; F: 202-895-1104

Toured, The: The Other Side of Tourism in Barbados
1993; 38 mins.; 16 mm; VHS

This documentary looks at some problems of tourism from the country being toured. It shows the realities of making a living and seeing your country's culture change under the pressures of the visitors. It deals with stereotypical ugly Americans and the government pressure to be tourist-friendly.

Center for Media and Independent Learning, 2000 Center Street, 4th Floor, Berkeley, CA 94704
P: 510-642-0460; F: 510-643-9271; e-mail: cmil@uclink.berkeley.edu

Transnational Fiesta: 1992

1993; 61 mins.; 16 mm; VHS

Indigenous cultures have been reasserting themselves in the Americas. This documentary explores the multicultural and transnational experience of Peruvian Andean immigrants living in Washington, D.C. and returning to their hometown in Peru to sponsor the annual fiesta.
Center for Media and Independent Learning, 2000 Center Street, 4th Floor, Berkeley, CA 94704
P: 510-642-0460; F: 510-643-9271; e-mail: cmil@uclink.berkeley.edu

Trekking on Tradition

1993; 45 mins.; 16 mm; VHS

This award-winning film illustrates the impact of trekking on a rural area in Nepal. It is viewed by both the trekkers (Europeans and Americans) and the Nepalese.
Center for Media and Independent Learning, 2000 Center Street, 4th Floor, Berkeley, CA 94704
P: 510-642-0460; F: 510-643-9271; e-mail: cmil@uclink.berkeley.edu

Uncommon Ground

1995; 57 mins.; 16 mm; VHS

Five multiethnic Los Angeles teens travel to South Africa to live with South African students in a black township. The film focuses on their personal experiences and incorporates the video diaries of each of the teens. The students share their experiences of family, school, violence, racism, and oppression.
New Day Films, 22-D Hollywood Avenue, Hohokus, NJ 07423
P: 201-652-6590; F: 201-652-1973; e-mail: tmcndy@aol.com

Understanding House and Apartment Rental in America

1989; 17 mins.; VHS

This program helps viewers understand the monetary and legal obligations they will assume when they agree to rent a house or apartment and the consequences they may face if they do not make rent payments promptly. Good tenants have rights of which they should be aware. Renters' rights and the role of the manager are explained. (Part of the Newcomers to America series; available in fifteen languages.)
Newcomers to America, PO Box 339, Portland, OR 97207
P: 800-776-1610; F: 503-241-3507

University Lecture, The: Four Teaching Styles

1987; 26 mins.; VHS

> Four teaching styles in the undergraduate classroom are described. The video is best used as a vehicle for discussion in the training of new teaching assistants or anyone else beginning a career as a university lecturer.
>
> Center for English as a Second Language, PO Box 210024, University of Arizona, Tucson, AZ 85721-0024
>
> P: 520-621-7063; F: 520-621-9180

Using Financial Services

1989; 19 mins.; VHS

> Newcomers often keep large amounts of money and valuables hidden in their homes. All too often, life savings and irreplaceable items are stolen. This program will introduce the basics of banking: savings accounts, check writing, safe deposit boxes, and car and home loan applications. How to establish a good line of credit is explained. (Part of the Newcomers to America series; available in fifteen languages.)
>
> Newcomers to America, PO Box 339, Portland, OR 97207
>
> P: 800-776-1610; F: 503-241-3507

Using Health Care Services

1989; 17 mins.; VHS

> Many newcomers are wary, fearful, and confused about some Western medical practices. Consequently, many who need treatment are reluctant to seek it. This program explores some of the features and common practices of American medicine, such as the availability of free or low-cost health care, how to find a doctor, what to expect during a physical exam, and how to use prescription medications safely. (Part of the Newcomers to America series; available in fifteen languages.)
>
> Newcomers to America, PO Box 339, Portland, OR 97207
>
> P: 800-776-1610; F: 503-241-3507

Using Your Hands to Teach Pronunciation

1995; 37 mins.; VHS

> This program demonstrates ways that teachers can help learners recognize target language features such as stress, intonation, rhythm, vowel length, voicing, aspiration, and the position of the tongue, teeth, and lips in articulating vowels and consonants, by providing a variety of cues with the hands.
>
> Sunburst Media, PO Box 61885, Sunnyvale, CA 94088-1885
>
> P: 408-245-8514; F: 408-245-8514; e-mail: sunburstm@aol.com

Victim of Two Cultures

1990; 52 mins.; VHS

Richard Rodriguez, in conversation with Bill Moyers, explains his opposition to bilingual education and talks about growing up in America as a child of immigrants.

Films for the Humanities and Sciences, PO Box 2053, Princeton, NJ 08543-2053

P: 800-257-5126; F: 609-275-3767

Vidioms: Activating Idioms for ESL

1991; 120 mins.; VHS

Students learn to use idioms with confidence in fifteen lessons. The duration of a lesson is short enough to permit two viewings in a single class period. There are usually three short skits per idiom.

Delta Systems, 1400 Miller Parkway, McHenry, IL 60050-7030

P: 800-323-8270; F: 800-909-9901

Voices of Challenge: Hmong Women in Transition

1996; 39 mins.; VHS

The women's stories begin when they are young girls in Laos. Their families are forced to flee in 1975. Surviving hunger and disease, they eventually settle in the U.S. These women provide insight into the Southeast Asian refugee experience and the changes facing them as they break from a traditional patriarchal family structure and assimilate into American society.

Carousel Film and Video, 280 Fifth Avenue, New York, NY 10001

P: 212-683-1660; F: 212-683-1662; e-mail: carousel@pipeline.com

Voices of Experience: Cross-Cultural Adjustment

1999; 38 mins.; VHS

This film showcases the stories of international businesspeople and students whose position in crossing cultures provides a view of adjustment to American life. Culture shock, personal change, teaching styles, homesickness, predeparture expectations, and value differences are covered. The film is designed for use by intensive English orientation programs, corporations preparing employees to work in the U.S., diversity training, and cross-cultural discussion.

The Seabright Group, Instructional Media, 216 F Street, Suite 25, Davis, CA 95616

P/F: 530-759-0684; e-mail: SeabrightG@davis.com

Waging Peace
1996; 56 mins.; VHS

> This film documents the Tomorrow's Leader Conference in Venice, Italy, sponsored by the Elie Wiesel Foundation for Humanity. Thirty teenagers from crisis areas around the world discuss conflict resolution techniques.
>
> Disney Educational Productions, 105 Terry Drive, Suite 120, Newtown, PA 18940
> P: 800-295-5010; F: 215-579-8589

Way We Are Living Now, The: Portraits of International Student Spouses
1989; 18 mins.; VHS

> Many challenges are faced by spouses of international students at U.S. campuses. Through a series of individual portraits from daily life, the video explores potential issues: overcoming isolation and language barriers, maintaining a marriage and raising children in a different culture, continuing one's education and career, and creating a new network of friends.
>
> NAFSA Publications, PO Box 1020, Sewickley, PA 15143
> P: 800-836-4994, F: 412-741-0609; e-mail: inbox@nafsa.org

Ways to Learn about Another Culture
1985; 6½ hrs.; VHS

> This unit in the International Communication series focuses on four specific techniques to gather and evaluate cross-cultural information: observing, participating, reflecting, and researching. The cases of a German and a Colombian exchange student are featured.
>
> Youth for Understanding Program Services, 3501 Newark Street, NW, Washington, DC 20016.
> P: 800-424-3691, ext. 134; F: 202-895-1104

Welcome to Canada
1989; 87 mins.; VHS

> This film chronicles the illegal landing of a boatload of Sri Lankan Tamils on Canada's east coast. They are rescued from certain death by fishermen and find temporary sanctuary in an isolated fishing village in Newfoundland. This is a portrayal of an unusual encounter between two cultures worlds apart.
>
> Canadian Film Distribution Center, SUNY Plattsburgh, Feinberg Library, Plattsburgh, NY 12901-2697
> P: 800-388-6784; F: 518-564-2112

What Is Expected of Foreign Graduate Students in the U.S.

1982; 13 mins.; VHS

This video, produced by Gary Althen at the University of Iowa, remains useful in acquainting new foreign graduate students with the intellectual skills and study habits needed for success in U.S. graduate education.

NAFSA Publications, PO Box 1020, Sewickley, PA 15143

P: 800-836-4994; F: 412-741-0609; e-mail: inbox@nafsa.org

When Cultures Meet Face to Face: The Intercultural Experience

1986; 30 mins.; VHS

Designed for intercultural learning at college campuses, high schools, and some work settings, this training tool can be used to sensitize Americans who interact with members of the international community or vice versa. It includes a training booklet.

Penfield Associates, PO Box 4493, Highland Park, NJ 08904

P: 908-932-7496, ext. 121; e-mail: penfield@rci.rutgers.edu

When Mrs. Hegarty Comes to Japan

1992; 58 mins.; 16 mm; VHS

Filmmaker Noriko Sekiguchi documents her "adopted" Australian mother's visit to Japan. She examines cross-cultural exchange, shows quirky juxtapositions, generation gaps, and diverse outlooks on life.

First Run/Icarus Films, 153 Waverly Place, 6th Floor, New York, NY 10014

P: 212-727-1711; F: 212-255-7923; e-mail: mail@frif.com

Who Is a Real Canadian?

1994; 25 mins.; VHS

This film looks at the growing diversity of Canada and documents the clash between official multiculturalism and the practical aspects of living with diversity.

Canadian Film Distribution Center, SUNY Plattsburgh, Feinberg Library, Plattsburgh, NY 12901-2697

P: 800-388-6784; F: 518-564-2112

Work beyond the Classroom

1990; 48 mins.; VHS

This documentary on the trials, tribulations, and truths discovered in professional and academic work outside the classroom features U.S. Fulbright professors in Thailand, Malaysia, and Indonesia. It is sponsored by the U.S. Fulbright Program, and is produced by North State Public Video.

Dr. Pamela George, Professor of Educational Psychology, School of Education, North Carolina Central University, Durham, NC 27707

P: 919-560-5175; e-mail: pggeorge@nccu.edu

Working with Americans: Leadership

1998; 26 mins.; VHS

This video focuses on ways in which Asians can work more effectively with their North American colleagues, giving practical recommendations for establishing credibility and making effective presentations. It teaches how to convey the proper level of confidence through both nonverbal and verbal behaviors such as eye contact, asking questions, and checking for understanding.

Meridian Resources Associates, 1741 Buchanan Street, San Francisco, CA 94115

P: 800-626-2047; F: 415-749-0124

Working with China

1996; 3 hrs.; VHS

This series of six videos introduces skills and strategies for effectively interacting and negotiating with the Chinese. Through dramatizations and interviews with expatriates and managers in the field, the sequences deal with matters such as communication barriers, understanding rank and titles, developing *guanxi* (connections), and Chinese views of contracts, law, protocol and protecting proprietary information.

Meridian Resources Associates, 1741 Buchanan St., San Francisco, CA 94115

P: 800-626-2047; F: 415-749-0124

Working with Japan

1993; 4^1/$_2$ hrs.; VHS

This series of seven videos, through depiction of negotiations between U.S. and Japanese business executives, illustrates Japanese values and behaviors, comparative business styles, socializing, handling stereotypes, and building relationships. Realistic business scenarios provide practical advice for cultivating productive interaction with Japanese counterparts.

Meridian Resources Associates, 1741 Buchanan Street, San Francisco, CA 94115

P: 800-626-2047; F: 415-749-0124

World at Work, The

1996; 16 mins.; VHS

This video introduces concepts of employment and the workplace, how they are culturally different, and typical assumptions of people entering the job market. Knowing how the job market works in America will provide newcomers with a competitive advantage in finding employment. (Part of the Newcomers to America series; available in eight languages.)

Newcomers to America, PO Box 339, Portland, OR 97207

P: 800-776-1610; F: 503-241-3507

World in Balance, The: A Health Orientation for New Foreign Students

1995; 15 mins.; VHS

Many international students are unfamiliar with the U.S. health care system's fee-for-service approach. They are often confused by the concepts of health insurance, specialized medicine, and high hospital costs. They may even be intimidated by lengthy medical forms and the idea of a routine physical examination. This video orients foreign college students to the U.S. health care system, following several students from home to class and to their health care providers.

NAFSA Publications, PO Box 1020, Sewickley, PA 15143

P: 800-836-4994; F: 412-741-0609; e-mail: inbox@nafsa.org

World of Differences: Understanding Cross-Cultural Communication

1997; 30 mins.; VHS

This program shows how successful cross-cultural communication can be when we understand differences in language, values, gestures, rituals, and traditions. It deals with the many things that set cultures apart and make them unique.

Center for Media and Independent Learning, 2000 Center Street, 4th Floor, Berkeley, CA 94704

P: 510-642-0460; F: 510-643-9271; e-mail: cmil@uclink.berkeley.edu

World of Gestures, A

1991; 26 mins.; 16 mm; VHS

This program explores the meanings and emotions of gestures around the world. It features students from sixteen countries performing their native gestures. In commentary between segments, an American professor adds perspective using American gestures. A teacher's guide is available.

Center for Media and Independent Learning, 2000 Center Street, 4th Floor, Berkeley, CA 94704

P: 510-642-0460; F: 510-643-9271; e-mail: cmil@uclink.berkeley.edu

World Song
1992; 15 mins.; VHS

A kaleidoscope of images and cross-cultural songs celebrating our common humanity, the program focuses on everyday events in the lives of people from different cultures of the world. Successive generations break bread around the dinner table, and families witness first love, marriage, birth, and aging.

Pyramid Film and Video, PO Box 1084, Santa Monica, CA 90406-1048

P: 800-421-2304; F: 310-453-9083; e-mail: info@pyramedia.com

World within Reach: A Predeparture Orientation Resource for Exchange and Education Abroad Programs
1995; 55 mins.; VHS

This instructional video is a predeparture orientation tool for students considering studying abroad. It features anecdotes and advice, wisdom and warnings, and experience and encouragement from people who have been abroad and have returned to share their sometimes hard-earned knowledge. The five modules are: predeparture preparation, academic environment, host culture awareness, culture shock, and coming back home. Accompanied by a user's guide.

WSAnet Ontario, International Centre, Queen's University, Kingston, ON K7L 3N6, Canada

P: 613-533-2604: F: 613-533-6190; e-mail: sales@quic.queensu.ca

Wrong Idea, The: A Cross-Cultural Training Program about Sexual Harassment
1989; 20 mins.; VHS

This video is designed to sensitize American and international students, faculty, and staff to the cultural and gender issues surrounding sexual harassment, as well as to their legal rights and responsibilities. Nine vignettes portray campus sexual harassment incidents through the use of culturally diverse cases. The video is accompanied by a training manual.

NAFSA Publications, PO Box 1020, Sewickley, PA 15143

P: 800-836-4994; F: 412-741-0609; e-mail: inbox@nafsa.org

Yeah, You Rite!
1984; 28 mins.; VHS

We are provided with a humorous look at the variety of ethnic and cultural differences in the speech and local dialects of residents of New Orleans.

The Center for New American Media, 524 Broadway, 2nd Floor, New York, NY 10012

P: 212-925-5665

Yellow Tale Blues: Two American Families

1990; 30 mins.; VHS

In this documentary on ethnic stereotypes, clips from Hollywood movies—from a vintage 1910 silent film to *Breakfast at Tiffany's*—reveal nearly a century of disparaging images of Asians. These familiar images are juxtaposed with portraits of the Choys, an immigrant working-class family, and the Tajimas, a fourth-generation middle-class California family.

Filmakers Library, Inc., 124 East 40th Street, New York, NY 10016

P: 212-808-4980; F: 212-808-4983; e-mail: info@filmakers.com

Your Cultural Passport to International Business

1995; 28 mins.; VHS

Awareness of cultural differences makes good sense when business crosses cultural boundaries. This video examines some cultural differences and how they can affect communication.

Meridian Education, 236 Front Street, Bloomington. IL 60701

P: 800-727-5507; F: 309-829-8621

Feature Films

Ah Ying (*Banbianren*)

1983; 110 mins.

Made in Hong Kong, this is a multilingual film in which both the conflict of cultures and the conflict of languages play a part. Ah Ying explores the lives of two people from two very different Chinese worlds: a young Hong Kong working-class woman and a northern Chinese film artist trained in the U.S. *Banbianren*, the original Mandarin title of the film, sums up the sense of the characters' alienation. It means "the person who half belongs." (In Cantonese and Mandarin with English subtitles.)

Alamo Bay

1985; 99 mins.

This American film, directed by Louis Malle, provides a tale of contemporary racism, pitting an angry Vietnam veteran against a Vietnamese refugee who, he feels, threatens his livelihood as a fisherman. Set in a Texas port, the film's development leads inexorably to the revival of the Ku Klux Klan.

Alice in the Cities

1974; 110 mins.

This German film shows an alienated journalist wandering aimlessly across America, who finds himself saddled with a nine-year-old girl. It reflects on the effect of American pop culture on postwar Europeans.

Assignment, The

1977; 94 mins.

This Swedish film portrays the drama of a Swedish diplomat who is sent to mediate a turbulent political situation in Latin America.

Babette's Feast

1987; 102 mins.

Based on a short story by Isak Dinesen, this film is about fine dining and the juxtaposition of Danish and French culture. Two spinsters, daughters of a minister in a remote Jutland community, take in a Parisian refugee and experience the wizardry of her gastronomic talents.

Ballad of Gregorio Cortez, The
1983; 99 mins.

Set at the turn of the twentieth century, this film is based on one of the most famous manhunts in Texas history. It is the story of a Mexican farmhand who killed a Texas sheriff in self-defense and tried to escape the law, all because of a mistranslation and a misunderstanding of the Spanish language, raising issues of stereotyping and prejudice.

Beyond the Plains
1977; 52 mins.

This story of the son of a Masai herdsman documents his transition from the nomadic life of the Masai people to his emergence, through state-required education, as a university professor. His evolution from Masai to Tanzanian parallels the growth and development of the Tanzanian nation and the African continent.

Bombay Talkie
1970; 110 mins.

A best-selling American woman novelist arrives in India seeking experience for her writing and gets romantically involved with an Indian movie star. (A James Ivory/Ismail Merchant production.)

Bread and Chocolate
1973; 112 mins.

This tragicomedy depicts an Italian guest worker in Switzerland desperately trying to break into the host culture. (In Italian with English subtitles.)

Bwana Toshi
1965; 115 mins.

This Japanese film, made on location in East Africa, shows the misunderstandings which people of different cultures have to learn to overcome before they can achieve goodwill. (In Japanese with English subtitles; now out of print, it may be difficult to locate.)

Chan Is Missing
1981; 80 mins.

A black-and-white film set in San Francisco, the story follows the search by two Chinese American cab drivers for their missing business partner, a middle-aged Taiwan immigrant who has vanished with their $2000. The process humorously leads to penetrating revelations about cultural identities.

Chocolat

1988; 105 mins.

A French woman who grew up in Cameroon remembers her childhood experiences surrounding the unfulfilled sexual tension between her mother and the black houseboy she befriended. This French film, in French with English subtitles, shows the cultural separation between the French colonials and the Africans they dominated.

City of Joy

1992; 134 mins.

A cynical American surgeon living in Calcutta finds himself after being involved with a health clinic for the poor. There are segments on contrasts in attitudes and levels of material comfort.

Coca-Cola Kid, The

1985; 94 mins.

A market researcher is sent to Australia to boost sales of Coca-Cola. He runs into problems with his amorous secretary, his resemblance to a CIA agent, and a home-grown soda entrepreneur.

Combination Platter

1993; 84 mins.

A young illegal immigrant from Hong Kong toils in a New York Chinese restaurant and learns that U.S. citizenship may mean having to marry an American. The film includes discussions of immigration problems.

Deep Blue Night

1983; 93 mins.

Filmed on location in the U.S., this Korean film (with English subtitles) traces the career of a young Korean who marries to get a green card after abandoning his first American lover in Death Valley.

Dersu Uzala

1975; 124 mins.

This acclaimed, photographically breathtaking film is about a Russian surveyor in Siberia who befriends a crusty, resourceful Mongolian. They begin to teach each other about their respective worlds. (Directed by Akira Kurosawa; produced in Russia.)

Dim Sum

1985; 88 mins.

This is the second independent film from the director of *Chan Is Missing*. A Chinese American mother and daughter living in San Francisco's Chinatown confront the conflict between traditional Eastern ways and modern American life. When a fortune-teller predicts the mother's death, the mother steps up efforts to convince her daughter to marry a boyfriend, while the daughter grapples with her filial responsibilities.

Dragon Chow

1987; 75 mins.

This German film, presented in German, Urdu, and Mandarin with English subtitles, is the story of two resourceful refugees, one Pakistani and the other Chinese, who meet in Hamburg and decide to take matters into their own hands by opening a restaurant.

El Norte

1983; 140 mins.

After a military massacre of laborers in Guatemala, Enrique takes his sister Rosa to head for the fabled land of opportunity north of Mexico. The film unfolds through their efforts to cross illegally into the U.S. and the ensuing hardships and cultural adjustments to survive.

Fear Eats the Soul

1974; 90 mins.

This film from Germany, dealing with xenophobia, is the story of a doomed love affair between a 60-year-old German cleaning woman and a black Moroccan immigrant worker. Racial prejudice and moral hypocrisy within modern German society are portrayed. (Directed by Rainer Werner Fassbinder.)

Foreign Student, The

1994; 93 mins.

An African American female teacher/domestic becomes romantically involved with a Parisian male studying at a small rural college in the 1950s. Race, class, and value systems are in conflict.

Foreigners (*Jag Heter Stelius*)

1972; 113 mins.

This film from Sweden (titled *Jag Heter Stelius* in Swedish) tells about the experiences of Greek immigrants in egalitarian Sweden, scripted from a novel based on the author's own experiences.

Gaijin: A Brazilian Odyssey

1979; 105 mins.

A young Japanese woman tells of her journey from Japan to Brazil at the turn of the twentieth century along with 800 of her countrymen. Seeking wealth on the coffee plantations, they experience, instead, isolation, exploitation, and demoralization as "gaijin," or outsiders. Many scenes illustrate the clash of Brazilian and Japanese cultures.

Great Wall, A

1986; 103 mins.

An upper-class Chinese American family (the father is a computer executive) returns to the country of its roots, only to face unforeseen cultural differences with the Chinese relatives and the experience of real culture shock. This was the first American feature film shot in China.

Green Card

1990; 108 mins.

A young woman agrees to marry a Frenchman, in name only, so he may legally remain in the U.S. There are stereotypes of the French and questions about attitudes toward immigrants.

Gung Ho

1985; 111 mins.

A Japanese firm takes over a small-town Pennsylvania auto factory, causing major cultural difficulties. Straining to contain U.S. workers' resentment, the foreman has to smooth over the introduction of streamlined practices and zero-defect efficiency. A walkout threatens the future of the partnership, but comic situations and an upbeat ending prevail.

Guru, The

1968; 112 mins.

James Ivory film features Michael York as a 1960s pop idol who journeys to India for sitar lessons, providing incongruous cultural collisions while displaying Indian lifestyles.

Heat and Dust

1982; 130 mins.

A James Ivory production adapted by Ruth Prawer Jhabvala from her own novel, this British film deals with themes like the exoticism of India stirring English blood, the past hanging heavy over the present, and dirty dealings flourishing behind a cloak of good manners. A young bride joins her husband at his post in India and is inexorably drawn to the country and its Prince of State.

Iron and Silk

1991; 92 mins.

A Yale graduate goes to China to teach English and gets educated by everyone he encounters. The film is filled with useful scenes of an American learning Chinese ways—education, martial arts, food, dance, and music.

Joy Luck Club, The

1993; 135 mins.

Here is an interweaving of eight stories: the saga of four women who survived their growing up in China and the clashes with their assimilated American daughters. Scenes of interaction include a lecture on Chinese table manners, glimpses of expectations, and prejudice.

Last Wave, The

1978; 103 mins.

An Australian attorney takes on a murder case involving an Aborigine. He finds himself becoming distracted by apocalyptic visions concerning tidal waves and drownings that seem to foretell the future. The film depicts the conflicts that arise between two culturally diverse societies.

Lawrence of Arabia

1962; 221 mins.

This is a famous epic biography of T. E. Lawrence, who took it upon himself as a British "observer" to strategically aid the Arab Bedouin in battling the Turks.

Living on Tokyo Time

1986; 85 mins.

This U.S. film follows the story of a young Japanese woman who visits the U.S., leaving behind a broken engagement at home and who, after her visa expires, marries a rock and roll musician. Issues of language and cultural differences between Japanese and Japanese Americans are explored.

Milagro Beanfield War, The

1988; 118 mins.

This adaptation of the John Nichols novel portrays a New Mexican village threatened by development and how a single act of rebellion rekindles its pride and strength of spirit. The cultural confrontation between outside Anglo developers and resident Latinos pervades the sometimes magical plot.

Mission, The
1986; 25 mins.

This historical drama about Jesuit missions in the Brazilian rain forest in the eighteenth century shows how these missions were eliminated by the legalized slave trading of Portugal. The film recounts the lives of two men, one a Jesuit priest, the other a slave trader turned priest, who deal with the injustice differently, one through prayer and the other through violence. These differing European confrontations with the Indian population raise cross-cultural issues.

Mississippi Masala
1991; 110 mins.

This story of an interracial romance between an African American man and a transplanted Indian woman from Uganda depicts the problems the liaison causes their families and their respective communities.

Mosquito Coast, The
1986; 119 mins.

This adaptation of the Paul Theroux novel chronicles the adventures of a sociopathic inventor as he moves his family to a Central American rain forest with the fateful intention of creating an aboriginal utopia.

My American Cousin
1985; 95 mins.

This story takes place in British Columbia in the summer of 1959 and deals with a girl's infatuation with her California cousin. It presents some subtleties of cultural differences among English-speaking peoples.

My Father Is Coming
1991; 82 mins.

A young German actor in New York is searching for someone to love, when her father comes to visit. The film deals with sorting out identity via cultural interaction.

Passage to India, A
1984; 65 mins.

An Academy Award-winning epic based on the classic E. M. Forster novel, this sweeping view of India in 1928 explores the treatment of Indians at the hands of the ruling British. A young British woman who befriends an Indian doctor later accuses him of attempted rape after a strange incident at India's Malabar Caves.

Perfumed Nightmare
1977; 93 mins.

This film from the Philippines, in Tagalog and English with English subtitles, presents a semiautobiographical fable about a young Filipino and his awakening to, and reaction against, American cultural colonialism. It is the story of the journey of Kidlat Tahimik from a small Philippine village, where he is the president of the local Wernher von Braun fan club, to Paris, where he goes to run a chewing gum franchise.

Pushing Hands
1992; 100 mins.

When a Chinese American brings his father, a non-English-speaking tai chi master, to live with him and his American wife and son in a New York suburb, cross-cultural conflicts ensue.

Ready to Wear
1994; 133 mins.

This rather plotless depiction of the French fashion industry, as it descends on Paris for the annual shows, contains some significant stereotypes of both French and American behavior.

Rhapsody in August
1991; 98 mins.

Directed by the famed Akira Kurosawa, this film reveals the memories of a Japanese grandmother, who recalls the horrors of the Nagasaki bombing, and her Japanese American grandson, who raises issues of reconciliation and pain.

Rising Sun
1993; 129 mins.

A Los Angeles cop and a Japanese criminal expert investigate a homicide that implicates a large Japanese corporation and a U.S. senator. There are issues of racial stereotyping and fears of Japanese business methods useful for discussion.

Shadowlands
1993; 130 mins.

This story of C. S. Lewis, portrayed as a rigid Oxford don, and his romance with an American poet shows cultural conflicts and may be useful for orientation to British life.

Small Pleasures

1993; 86 mins.; 35 mm; VHS

This feature film shows two young women immigrants to Toronto who move from China in the fateful Tiananmen spring of 1989. One embraces everything new with enthusiasm while the other is less sure about the value of Western ideas. Through a series of survival experiences and romantic situations while going to school, they experience heartache but remain friends and find a way to live in a Western country.

Wondrous Light, Inc., 174 Fulton Avenue, Toronto, ON M4K 1Y3, Canada
P: 416-429-7399; F: 416-696-9108; e-mail: klock@pathcom.com

Soursweet

1988; 112 mins.

This British film relates the experiences of a Hong Kong couple who start a new life in London. Culture shock examples are provided for different generations. Working as a waiter, Chen escapes to anonymity in the East End to avoid being entangled with drug running. Chinatown gang feuds prevail.

Swissmakers, The

1978; 108 mins.

This lighthearted satire, a humane parody of cuckoo-clock Switzerland, has an amiable young bureaucrat snooping on immigrants to see if they are "suitable" for Swiss citizenship. (In Swiss-German with English subtitles.)

36 Chowringhee Lane

1982; 122 mins.

An elderly teacher in Calcutta welcomes a young couple into her home and discovers a newfound sense of family, which is abruptly shattered when the couple marry and leave. This story of loneliness offers a glimpse of the British in India after the fall of the British empire.

Ugly American, The

1963; 120 mins.

Based upon the William J. Lederer novel, the film deals with a naive American ambassador to a small civil-war-torn Asian country who must fight a miniature cold war against northern Communist influence.

Walkabout
1971; 95 mins.

Two English children abandoned in the Australian outback when their father commits suicide are found by a young Aborigine boy. The three enjoy life in an unspoiled primitive world until civilization intrudes.

Wedding Banquet, The
1993; 111 mins.

A gay Taiwanese American (whose parents are about to visit), his lover, and a Chinese woman in search of a green card concoct a fake wedding for the arriving parents. Homosexuality and cross-cultural issues invade the same scenario.

Wedding in Galilee
1986; 116 mins.

This is a multilayered portrayal of conflicts among villagers, family, and Israelis, when the Arab *muktar* of a Palestinian village under Israeli occupation invites the Israeli military governor to be guest of honor at the traditional wedding ceremony of his son.

Zorba the Greek
1964; 142 mins.

A British writer and a Greek opportunist on Crete take lodgings with an aging courtesan. The writer is attracted to a woman who is stoned by the villagers when they find he has spent the night with her. Based on the novel by Nikos Kazantzakis, this now classic film portrays the cultural responses by an Anglo-Saxon to his new Mediterranean environment.

Appendix

Documentary Titles by Category

Animation

Balablok
Chairy Tale, A
Stereotypes

Business Communication

American Business English
Building the Transnational Team
Cultural Diversity: At the Heart of Bull
Doing Business in Asia
Doing Business in Japan
Doing Business in Latin America
Doing Business in Southeast Asia
Doing Business in Vietnam
Global One: The Art and Science of Global Success
Globally Speaking: Skills and Strategies for Success in Asia
Going International: Managing the Overseas Assignment
Going International: Working in the U.S.A.
How to Welcome Business Visitors from Japan
International Business Practices
Managing Cultural Differences
Managing Cultural Synergy
Managing in China
Negotiating in Today's World
West Meets East: In Japan
Working with Americans: Leadership
Working with China
Working with Japan
Your Cultural Passport to International Business

Community Volunteers

Home Is in the Heart: Accommodating Persons with Disabilities into the Homestay
Hosting with AFS
Open Homes, Open Hearts: Hosting International Students
Way We Are Living Now, The: Portraits of International Student Spouses
When Cultures Meet Face to Face: The Intercultural Experience
Working Together

Cross-Cultural Learning

Across Cultures
Better Together Than A-P-A-R-T
Bias Awareness in a Multicultural World
Blue-Eyed
Body Language: An International View
Chinese Cultural Values: The Other Pole of the Human Mind
Clothing—A Cross-Cultural Study, Parts 1 and 2
Color Schemes
Cross-Cultural Communication in Diverse Settings
Cross-Cultural Communications
Cross-Cultural Comparisons
Cross-Cultural Comparisons, Continued
Cross-Cultural Differences in Newborn Behavior
Cross-Cultural Problem Solving
Cross-Purposes
Cultural Baggage
Cultural Diversity: Meeting the Challenge
Culture: What Is It?
Cultures around the World
Cultures: Similarities and Differences
Dance and Human History
Desi Remix Chicago Style
Developing a Dual Perspective
Different Place, A, *and* Creating Community
Doubles: Japan and America's Intercultural Children
Dull Guys, The
Families
Family across the Sea
Food—A Cross-Cultural Study, Parts 1 and 2
For Our Bread
Four Families

From Freak Street to Goa
Global Groove
Global One: The Art and Science of Global Success
Going International: Beyond Culture Shock
Going International: Bridging the Culture Gap
Housing—A Cross-Cultural Study, Parts 1 and 2
How Beliefs and Values Define a Culture
How Economic Activities Define a Culture
How Geography Defines a Culture
How Social Organizations Define a Culture
Images That Speak: The Cross-Cultural Communications Workshop
In Praise of Hands
Invisible Walls
Islam and Puritanism
Jew in the Lotus, The
Kuro Kuro: A Portrait of Ethnocentrism and Cultural Relativity
Learning about Language
Learning to Hate
Letters Not about Love
Maceo: Demon Drummer from East L.A.
Made in China
Mah-Jongg Orphan
Mah-Jongg: The Tiles That Bind
Mosori Monika
Multicultural Incidents in Ten Zoos
Oasis of Peace
Palenque: Un Canto
Palm Play
People and Culture
Public Diplomacy
Rainbow War
Rassias in China
Reassemblage
Soviet Students Speak to America
Step Style
Stereotypes
Stereotyping (International Version)
Teaching the Chinese Student
To Live in a Multicultural World
Transnational Fiesta: 1992
Ways to Learn about Another Culture

When Cultures Meet Face to Face: The Intercultural Experience
Working Together
World of Differences: Understanding Cross-Cultural Communication
World of Gestures, A
Yeah, You Rite

Cultural Conflicts within the United States

A-M-E-R-I-C-A-N-S
Acting Our Age
Adjustment to a New Way of Life
Afterbirth
Americanization of Elias, The
Anatomy of a Spring Roll
Be Good, My Children
Becoming American
Between Two Worlds
Bittersweet Survival
Bittersweet: The Asian-Indian Experience in the USA
Blue-Collar and Buddha
Chief in Two Worlds, A
Chinese Cultural Values: The Other Pole of the Human Mind
Cold Water
Color of Fear, The
Columbus on Trial
Coming Across
Displaced in the New South
Ethnic Notions
Farewell to Freedom
Foreign Talk
Freckled Rice
Gerónimo: His Story
Green Card: An American Romance
Horizons and Homelands: Integrating Cultural Roots
Japan Bashing
Japanese American Women: A Sense of Place
Knowing Her Place
Mako
Mr. Ahmed
Misunderstanding China
Monterey's Boat People
Moving Mountains: The Story of Yiu Mien

My America (or Honk If You Love Buddha)
New Puritans, The: The Sikhs of Yuba City
New Year
Ourselves
Pak Bueng on Fire
Price You Pay, The
Refugee Women in America
Refugee Youth in America
Slaying the Dragon
Tanto Tiempo
Taxi-Vala/Autobiography
Telling It Like It Is: Reflections on Cultural Diversity
Victim of Two Cultures
Voices of Challenge: Hmong Women in Transition
Yellow Tale Blues: Two American Families

Cultural Interaction and Conflicts

All Dressed in White
Balablok
Black to the Promised Land
Brighter Moon, A
Chairy Tale, A
Class Divided, A
Corporate Warrior
Crosstalk
Cultural Diversity: At the Heart of Bull
Do Two Halves Really Make a Whole?
Doing Business in Japan
Fishing in the City
From Here, from This Side
Homecoming
Korea: Homes Apart
Leaving Bakul Bagan
Migrant's Heart, A
Miles from the Border
Mott to Mulberry
My Country Left Me
Nirvana in Nova Scotia
Oaxacalifornia
People and Culture
Reassemblage

SST Office
Goshen College
Goshen, IN 46526

Search for Peking Dog
Small Pleasures
So Far from India
Thanh's War
To Canada: With Love and Some Misgivings
Toured, The: The Other Side of Tourism in Barbados
Trekking on Tradition
Uncommon Ground
Welcome to Canada
Who Is a Real Canadian?
World Song

Disabilities

Emerging Leaders
Home Is in the Heart: Accommodating Persons with Disabilities into the Homestay
Looking Back, Looking Forward
Mi Casa Es Su Casa (Let My Home Be Your Home)

Educating New Immigrants

Adjustment to a New Way of Life
Communicating Survival
Cultural Diversity: Meeting the Challenge
Culture Clash and the Law in America
Discrimination in the Workplace
Family Law in America
Finding a Job in America
Fishing, Hunting, and Firearms
Good Neighbors
Here to Help: The Police in America
How to Avoid Crime in America
In a Strange Land: Police and the Southeast Asian Refugee
Introduction to American Law
Introduction to American Public Schools
Job Search, The: A Cultural Orientation
Little Street Wisdom, A
Living in a Consumer Society
Motor Vehicles and the Law
People and Culture
Price You Pay, The

Refugee Women in America
Refugee Youth in America
So You Have a New Job
Understanding House and Apartment Rental in America
Using Financial Services
Using Health Care Services
World at Work, The

English-as-a-Second-Language Instruction

Accent Reduction
American Business English
American Scenes
Authentic American Activities
Body Language: An International View
Building Bridges to Friendship
Conversational Style in the USA
Conversational Styles around the Globe
English as a Second Language
Follow Me to America
Follow Me to San Francisco
In America
In English
In English on Your Own
Inside America: Scenes of Everyday Life
Learning English
Lost Secret 2000
Now You're Talking: English for Daily Living
Perfect English Pronunciation
Phrase by Phrase Pronunciation Videotapes
Pronunciation Workout for Foreign Language Learners
Real America, The: Scenes of Everyday Life
Real Thing, The
Sailing through English
Speak to Me
Speaking American English at Work
Stage One: The Natural Approach to Speaking English
Success Video Packages
Success with English
Vidioms: Activating Idioms for ESL

English-as-a-Second-Language Methodology

Breaking the Accent Barrier
Conversational Styles in the USA
Conversational Styles around the Globe
Good Evening, Teacher
Language Encounters of the Best Kind: Mainstreaming the E.S.L. Student
Language Teaching in Action: Videos for Teacher Training, #1—Grammar
Strategies for Educators: Teaching Hispanic Students
Teacher Training through Video: E.S.L. Techniques
Teaching the Chinese Student
Using Your Hands to Teach Pronunciation

Health

College Students and AIDS
Communicating Survival
House of the Spirit
Other Side of Winter, The
Using Health Care Services
World in Balance, The: A Health Orientation for New Foreign Students

International Youth

AFS Diversity Initiative, The
AFS Experience, The: Parent Focus
AFS Experience, The: Student Focus
Direct Connection
High School of American Dreams
Hosting with AFS
In Our Classroom
Journeys: AFS Adventures in Latin America
Planting Seeds for Peace
Soviet Students Speak to America
Waging Peace

Orientation to Living in the United States

After the Cult: Recovering Together
American Scenes
American Tongues
Building Bridges to Friendship
Cold Water

Communicating Survival
Cults: Saying No under Pressure
Culture Clash and the Law in America
Discrimination in the Workplace
Dormitory Diversity: Developing Cultural Awareness and Language Skills
East to West
Ethnic Notions
Family Law in America
Finding a Job in America
Fishing, Hunting, and Firearms
Going International: Living in the U.S.A.
Going International: Working in the U.S.A.
Good Neighbors
Here to Help: The Police in America
Hot Water: Intercultural Issues between Women and Men
How to Avoid Crime in America
Introduction to American Law
Introduction to American Public Schools
Job Search, The: A Cultural Orientation
Leaving Home: The American Experience of Six International Students
Little Street Wisdom, A
Living in a Consumer Society
Motor Vehicles and the Law
Other Side of Winter, The
Refugee Women in America
Refugee Youth in America
Sing a Song Together
So You Have a New Job
Talk to Me: Americans in Conversation
Understanding House and Apartment Rental in America
Using Financial Services
Using Health Care Services
Voices of Experience: Cross-Cultural Adjustment
Way We Are Living Now, The: Portraits of International Student Spouses
World at Work, The
Wrong Idea, The: A Cross-Cultural Training Program about Sexual Harassment

Orientation to Other Countries

American Game: Japanese Rules
Before You Pack: Preparing for Study in Africa
Black to the Promised Land

Bonds of Pride, The
Building Bridges to Friendship
EuropeBOUND
Favourable Exchange: International Students in Canada
Going International: Beyond Culture Shock
Going International: Managing the Overseas Assignment
Going International Safely
How Far Are You Willing to Go to Make a Difference?
International Assignment
Introduction to the Arab World
Islam and Christianity
Islam and Puritanism
Japanese Version, The
Jennifer's Chinese Diary
Korea: Homes Apart
Living in Africa: African Solutions to African Problems
Made in China
Making the Most of It
Managing Daily and University Life in China
Managing Daily and University Life in Southeast Asia, Part I: Making It Manageable
Managing Daily and University Life in Southeast Asia, Part II: Making It Meaningful
Planning for Study Abroad
Rassias in China
Remembering Wei Yi-fang, Remembering Myself
Solutions to Culture Stress
Struggle and Success
Study in Africa: New Opportunities for American Undergraduates
Study in Canada
Terra Cognita's Live Abroad
They Look at Your Face and See a Flag
When Mrs. Hegarty Comes to Japan
Work beyond the Classroom
World within Reach

Orientation to Study in the United States

Applying for the F-1 Student Visa at an American Consulate
F-1 Student Visas and Status in the U.S.
From Oh, No to OK: Communicating with Your Teaching Assistant
Leaving Home: The American Experience of Six International Students

Real Thing, The
Study in the U.S.: Engineering
Study in the U.S.: Graduate Medical Education
Study in the U.S.: Humanities and Social Sciences
What Is Expected of Foreign Graduate Students in the United States

Professional Development

Crosstalk
Cultural Crossings
Foreign Student Advising 101
From Survival to Adaptation: The Adolescent Refugee Experience
Images That Speak: The Cross-Cultural Communications Workshop
Outside the Classroom (or See Me during My Office Hours)
Paul Pedersen: Developing Multicultural Awareness
Peering Up

Reentry

After America...after Japan
Going International: Welcome Home Stranger
Professional Integration for a Smooth Passage Home
Returning Home: A Program for Re-entry
Solutions to Culture Stress
World within Reach

Safety and the Law

Communicating Survival
Culture Clash and the Law in America
Family Law in America
Fishing, Hunting, and Firearms
Going International Safely
Here to Help: The Police in America
How to Avoid Crime in America
In a Strange Land: Police and the Southeast Asian Refugee
Introduction to American Law
Little Street Wisdom, A
Motor Vehicles and the Law

Teaching Assistants

From Oh, No to OK: Communicating with Your Teaching Assistant
Outside the Classroom (or See Me during My Office Hours)
Techniques for Teachers: A Guide for Non-Native Speakers of English
University Lecture, The: Four Teaching Styles

Women's Issues

Abortion: Stories from North to South
I Am Your Sister
Ourselves
Refugee Women in America
Way We Are Living Now, The: Portraits of International Student Spouses